Anonymous

Directory of Licensed Real Estate Dealers of Chicago

1890-91

Anonymous

Directory of Licensed Real Estate Dealers of Chicago
1890-91

ISBN/EAN: 9783337067397

Printed in Europe, USA, Canada, Australia, Japan

Cover: Foto ©Suzi / pixelio.de

More available books at **www.hansebooks.com**

1890. 1891.

DIRECTORY

OF

LICENSED

Real Estate Dealers

AND BROKERS

OF

CHICAGO.

H
948
96
23

J. P. BISHOP,
REAL ESTATE

167 Dearborn Street, Suite 516,

STOCK EXCHANGE BUILDING, - CHICAGO.

Can Direct Parties to Big and Quick Paying Investments.

ACRES, LOTS AND BLOCKS.

Syndicates Organized and Property Subdivided.

REAL ESTATE BOUGHT, SOLD AND MANAGED ON COMMISSION.

FREDERICK T. HASKELL,
Mortgage Loans

203 STOCK EXCHANGE BUILDING,

167 DEARBORN STREET,
CHICAGO.

MORTGAGES BOUGHT AND SOLD.

BUILDING LOANS.

F. J. SPENCER.   A. C. FORDHAM.

SPENCER & FORDHAM,

REAL ESTATE

AND LOANS.

OFFICES:

Chamber of Commerce,   974 W. Madison Street,
ROOM 308.

TELEPHONE 2008.   TELEPHONE 7474.

MEMBERS REAL ESTATE BOARD.

CHICAGO,   -   ILLINOIS.

J. H. CURTIS.   C. H. MERRICK.

J. H. CURTIS & CO.

Real Estate Brokers

ROOM 28, REAPER BLOCK,

Cor. Washington and Clark Streets,

CHICAGO, ILLS.

We make the formation of Syndicates a Specialty.

The Syndicate plan allows small investors to combine their capital and purchase acres or other properties and handle them to as good advantage as a capitalist.

Small investors wishing to double their money in a short time are requested to communicate with us.

Owners of acres in Cook County, who will sell their land to Syndicates, on monthly payments, at regular market prices, are requested to list the same with us.

1890.   1891.

DIRECTORY

— OF —

Licensed Real Estate Dealers

OF CHICAGO.

INDEX.

Allen, Opdyke & Allen.. 39
Andrews A. H. & Co... 94
Aubert A. J..inside back cover
Barnes & Parish.. 13
Bartlett J. A... 17
Bartlett J. S. & Son...inside back cover
Bass, Kessler, Ennes & Co...left side lines
Bennett F. I. & Co... 7
Birge M. D. & Co.. 45
Bishop J. P..inside front cover
Bissinger Benj..right side lines
Bogue & Hoyt... 11
Boney Chas. M.. 94
Boyce & Kirwan... 45
Burge E. A... 23
Chamberlin Geo. W... 17
Chicago Union Lime Works... 15
Cleveland & Norton.. 35
Crocker & Sweet.. 25
Cronkrite B. F. & Co.. 33
Cronkrite Edward C. & Co......................................inside back cover
Culver B. F.. 5
Cummings E. A. & Co... 25
Cummings F. A. & Co... 23
Curtis J. H. & Co..front colored
Daly Hugh..top lines
Doland F. F. & Co.. 43
Dolese & Skeperd... 19
Drury Bros.. 53

4

WILLIAM REED. F. W. STUDDIFORD. R. R. YOUNT.

WILLIAM REED & CO.

REAL ESTATE AND LOANS,

1209 TACOMA BUILDING,

Corner La Salle and Madison Streets,

Telephone 5049. CHICAGO.

BELDEN F. CULVER,

REAL ESTATE AGENCY,

No. 59 DEARBORN STREET,

CHICAGO.

INDEX—Continued.

Dunning Andrew	53
Eggleston, Mallette & Brownell	31
Elliott, Mahon & Co.	27
Ellis John A.	55
Eulette C. H. & Co.	27
Galloway, Lyman & Patton	bottom lines
Garden City Sand Co. (The)	21
Gilliland L. O.	55
Graves Geo. M.	bottom lines and 41
Guthrie W.	37
Hammel & Lang	41
Hammond, Fry & Co.	top lines
Hansbrough Wm.	39
Haskell F. T.	inside front cover
Hoefer & Torpe	43
Hosmer & Fenn	63
Keith F. W. & Co	47
Kerrigan Jno. J	29
King S. T.	49
Kinkaid A. H.	47
Knefel John	49
Knight & Marshall	13
Kuehnau Carl V.	85
Leonard Mark T	57
Meckling J. S. & Co.	29
Metropolitan Investment Co.	outside back cover and 59
Monson & Smith	7
Moore E. B. & Co.	21
Ogden & Smith	51
Orr & Lockett	9
Palmer Chas. D. & Co.	51
Pratt & Ely	63
Preble & Co.	67
Radle, Jackson & Radle	65
Rand Chas. E.	89
Ratledge & Wright	65

FRANK I. BENNETT.   L. D. CORTRIGHT.   GEO. R. BENNETT.

FRANK I. BENNETT & CO.,
REAL ESTATE,

Buy, Sell and Rent Property of every description on commission.

ESTATES MANAGED.

Mortgage Loans Negotiated.

Special attention given to the interests of non-residents.

CORRESPONDENCE SOLICITED.

Office, N. W. Cor. Michigan Avenue and Jackson St.,

CHICAGO.

O. K. MONSON.   J. H. SMITH.

MONSON & SMITH,

REAL ESTATE,

Englewood Improved Property and South Side Acres
- - - a Specialty. - - -

MAIN OFFICE:

CHAMBER OF COMMERCE BUILDING, SUITE 416,

CHICAGO.

BRANCH OFFICE: · · · · · ·

642 SIXTY-THIRD STREET, ENGLEWOOD, ILLINOIS,

TELEPHONE 119.

INDEX—Continued.

Redfield C. S.	left side lines and backbone
Reed Wm. & Co.	5
Reynolds C. T.	69
Rice & Creighton.	69
Richards M. J.	75
Sampson J. C. & Co.	71
Sawyer & McFarland.	71
Schaar, Koch & Co.	inside back cover
Seymour Chas. A. & Co.	61
Shea D. W.	35
Short E. G. & Co.	67
Siddons Geo. S.	right side lines
Simpson Bros.	19
Spencer & Fordham	front colored
Stone John N. & Co.	79
Sturges, Barker & Betz.	75
Teed H. G. & Co.	57
United States Loan Syndicate (The)	83
Vail J. D. Jr.	81
Van Buren & Van Ston.	81
Van Keuren Chas. W	89
Watkins W. & Co.	15
Weinland Chas.	85
Whitney, Woodcock & Co.	87
Williams V. M. Co.	87
Wilson Walter H.	61

EXCLUSIVE SPECIALTIES IN FINE HARDWARE.

LARGEST ASSORTMENT AND LOWEST PRICES.

Builders' Hardware,

CUTLERY,

MECHANICS' TOOLS.

—SOLE AGENTS FOR—

The Norton Door Check and Spring,

Gardner's Steel Sash Ribbon and Pulleys,

Skidmore Adjustable Window Balcony.

For Cleaning the Outside of Windows of High Buildings.

OUR SPECIALTY IS BUILDERS' HARDWARE.

Owners, Architects and Contractors will be amply repaid by a visit to our store and an examination of our goods and prices before purchasing.

ORR & LOCKETT HARDWARE CO.

184 AND 186 CLARK STREET,

TELEPHONE 472. **CHICAGO, ILL.**

HUGH DALEY, 94 Washington St. Room 26. Telephone 2510. **Mortgage Loans**

(From May 1 to October 4, 1890, inclusive).

LICENSED REAL ESTATE DEALERS OF CHICAGO.

ABRAMS E. E.	203, 59 Dearborn
ACKERMANN HENRY	813 Division
ADAMS JAMES W.	**401, 85 Dearborn**
ADAMS W. H.	361, 63d
AHRENSFELD H. & CO.	23, 94 La Salle
ALCOTT J. B.	3848 State
ALDIS OWEN F.	707 Rookery
ALLEN EDWARD	**49, 79 Dearborn**
ALLEN, OPDYKE & ALLEN,	**29 and 30 Montauk blk.**
ALLEN, SYRETT & CO.	**516, 85 Dearborn**
ALLEN WM. T.	609, 87 Washington
ALMY & GARDNER	77 Clark
ALVENSLEBEN H. V.	452 Milwaukee av.
ALVORD W. P. & BERNDT	30, 94 La Salle
AMICK PLEASANT & FRANK S.	710 Chamber of Commerce bldg.
ANDERSON GUSTAVUS	153 Randolph
ANDERSON S. D.	354, 63d
ANNABLE S. L.	979 N. Clark
ANSON W. W. & CO.	115 Dearborn

C. S. REDFIELD, 620, 622, 218 La Salle St., **REAL ESTATE,** BARGAINS IN North Shore Property

BENJ. BISSINGER 122 La Salle St. **South Side Real Estate**

GALLOWAY, LYMAN & PATTON, Tacoma Building. | **REAL ESTATE** BOUGHT and SOLD ON COMMISSION.

GEORGE M. BOGUE.   HENRY W. HOYT.   HAMILTON B. BOGUE.

BOGUE & HOYT,

REAL ESTATE AGENCY

REAL ESTATE BOARD BUILDING,

N. E. Corner Dearborn and Randolph Sts.

TELEPHONE 830.

Real Estate Bought and Sold on Commission.

INVESTMENTS MADE FOR NON-RESIDENTS.

LOANS NEGOTIATED.

TAXES PAID AND RENTS COLLECTED.

CITY OF LONDON FIRE INS. CO. (Limited), ENGLAND.
HAMMOND, FRY & CO., Agts, 177 La Salle St. Tel. 465.

LICENSED REAL ESTATE DEALERS—Continued.

ATCHISON N	59, 90 Washington
AUBERT A. J	305 North av.
AUSTIN H. W.	43, 156 Lake
AUSTIN J. ALMON	6, 164 La Salle
AUSTIN & CO.	17, 182 Dearborn
AVERILL A. J.	619, 85 Dearborn
BACON JEREMIAH D.	69th, nw. cor. Winter
BACON J. K.	153 La Salle
BACON & CALKINS	316 Inter Ocean bldg.
BAILEY J. A. & CO.	725, 112 Clark
BAIRD & BRADLEY	90 La Salle
BAKER E. H.	Forest and Jackson av.
BAKER FRANCIS M.	34, 175 Dearborn
BAKER F. S.	43 and 44, 90 Washington
BAKER WILSON G.	33, 175 La Salle
BAKER W. M	200, 167 Dearborn
BAKER W. P.	210, 89 Washington
BALDWIN A. H. & CO.	9, 94 La Salle
BALDWIN BYRON A. & CO.	10 Borden blk.
BALDWIN HENRY	Riverside Ill.
BALLARD F. E. & CO.	601 Tacoma bldg.
BALSMYDER F. W.	403 Inter Ocean bldg.
BARBEE & BEATH	628, 69th
BARMM FRANK H. & CO.	21, 179 Washington
BARNARD F. C.	417 Chamber of Commerce bldg.
BARNARD M. R. & CO.	209 Opera House bldg.
BARNES NOAH	6, 85 Washington
BARNES & PARISH	157 La Salle
BARNETT I.	185 W. 14th
BARNEY J. A.	46, 88 Washington
BARRATT THEO. & WM.	133d and S. Chicago av.
BARTELS & SCHOEVERLING	460 S. Center av.

City and Suburban Property FOR SALE BY BASS, KESSLER, ENNES & CO. 108 Dearborn St. Rooms 33 & 34.

REAL ESTATE AND LOANS—GEO. S. SIDDONS, 48 & 50 Metropolitan B'k., 163 Randolph Street.

"Q" Real Estate | GEO. M. GRAVES, 406 Tacoma Bldg.

F. A. BARNES.   TELEPHONE 1931.   S. M. PARISH.

BARNES & PARISH,

Real Estate, Loan and Renting Agents.

STORES AND HOUSES RENTED.

Rents Collected, Estates Managed and Taxes Paid for Non-Residents.

157 La Salle St.,   CHICAGO.

JOHN B. KNIGHT.   JAMES M. MARSHALL.

ESTABLISHED 1854.

KNIGHT & MARSHALL,

Real Estate and Mortgage Loans

CHICAGO.

Special Attention Given to the Interests of Non-Residents.

HUGH DALEY, 94 Washington St. Room 26. Telephone 2510. **Property Rented**

South Evanston Real Estate, **C. S. REDFIELD,** 620/622 } 218 La Salle St.

BENJ. BISSINGER, 122 La Salle St. Real Estate and Loans

LICENSED REAL ESTATE DEALERS—Continued.

BARTLETT JOHN A......21, 152 La Salle
BARTLETT J. S. & SON.......5108 State
BARWICK JOHN.................10, 41 Clark
BASS, KESSLER, ENNES & CO. 33 and 34, 108 Dearborn
BATTCHER OSCAR ....760 N. Paulina
BAUMGARTL I. & CO.................332 W. 12th
BAY STATE REAL ESTATE AGENCY
 (C. W. Van Keuren, mngr.) 416, 70 State
BEACH, STONE & CO. 815 Chamber of Commerce bldg.
BEACHY ALBERT D. & CO. 319, 87 Washington
BEARDSLEY & BIVENS......406 Chamber of Commerce bldg.
BEAUREGARD & FLOWER............33, 125 Dearborn
BEDDOE H. R. & CO................150 Dearborn
BEES L. G. & CO..................101 Monroe
BEHNKE H. L. ....9850, 4th av.
BENEDICT O. L..........5, 125 Dearborn
BENNETT E. A. & CO......6, 59 Dearborn
BENNETT FRANK I. & CO. Michigan av. nw. cor. Jackson
BENNETT J. D. & CO...............150 La Salle
BENSON & PARSONS................16, 84 La Salle
BERGSTEDT C. G...................37, 156 Lake
BEST & BUCKLEY..................415, 85 Dearborn
BETTS WM ....79th nr. Bond av.
BIDGOOD WALTER H................30, 151 Monroe
BIGGS, PAUL G. & SON...31, 119 La Salle
BINGEMANN & CARTER..48, 125 Clark
BIRGE M. D. & CO..........146 La Salle

14

GALLOWAY, LYMAN & PATTON, Tacoma Building. | **Mortgage Loans FOR SALE**

W. WATKINS & CO.
Portland Cement Paving

SIDEWALKS A SPECIALTY.

Floors for Schools, Stables, Warehouses and Residences.

ALL WORK GUARANTEED.

Numerous References Given on Application.

Office: Room 47, 177 La Salle Street,

Box 22 Builders' Exchange.
TELEPHONE 406.

CHICAGO.

ESTABLISHED 1859.

Chicago Union Lime Works,

F. E. SPOONER, Agent.

Manufacturers of

Chicago Quick Lime,

McADAM AND CONCRETE

STONE.

Room 5, 159 La Salle St.,   CHICAGO.

TELEPHONE No. 234.

THE LONDON ASSURANCE CORPORATION (England.)
HAMMOND, FRY & CO., AGTS., 177 La Salle St. Tel. 465.

LICENSED REAL ESTATE DEALERS—Continued.

BIRKIN & PHILPOTT......................................197 State
BISHOP JOHN M......................................6340 Oglesby av
BISHOP J. D. & CO......................................89 Madison
BISHOP J. P..............516, 167 Dearborn
BISSELL & MANN......................................97, 175 Dearborn
BISSINGER BENJ..........9, 122 La Salle
BITTLESTON H. & CO. 56-57, 115 Dearborn
BLACK H. A......................................61, 97 Washington
BLOCKI E. W......................................4, 90 Washington
BLOSS S. M. & CO......................................47, 107 Dearborn
BLUHM OTTO......................................13 Montauk blk.
BLUM ROBERT J......................Graceland and Ashland avs.
BLUMENTHAL N. M. & CO......................29, 126 Washington
BODEN FRANK & CO......................................20, 195 La Salle
BOESENBERG H. H. & CO......................484 N. Ashland av.
BOGUE & HOYT..............59 Dearborn
BOLDENWECK WM......................728 Opera House bldg.
BOLGER THOMAS J......................................14, 99 Washington
BONNEY BROS..........511 Tacoma bldg.
Branch office 1054 Millard av.
BOOMER JOHN......................................19 Portland blk.
BOON & LANDWERR......................Michigan av. and 111th
BOOTH C. J. & CO......................................20, 94 La Salle
BOSWORTH A. O........805 Tacoma bldg.
BOUR GEO. C. & CO......................53d nw. cor. Lake av.
BOUTON S. F......................217 First National Bank bldg.
BOWERMAN, FARNUM & WARE......................83 Dearborn
BOWES ED. J., JR., & BRO......................44, 94 La Salle
BOWES & CRUICKSHANK..187 and 189 Dearborn
BOYCE & KIRWAN.64 and 65, 164 La Salle
BOYD T. B......................................128 La Salle

HOUSES AND LOTS in all parts of the city and suburbs, for sale by **BASS, KESSLER, ENNES & CO.** 108 Dearborn St., Rooms 33 & 34.

GEO. S. SIDDONS 48 & 50 Metropolitan Block, 163 Randolph Street, **Real Estate and Loans**

REAL ESTATE at HINSDALE | **GEO. M. GRAVES** 406 Tacoma Building.

J. A. BARTLETT.

REAL ESTATE,

LOANS,

NOTARY PUBLIC,

152 LA SALLE STREET,

Room 21 Otis Block. CHICAGO.

GEORGE W. CHAMBERLIN,

REAL ESTATE,

34, 99 WASHINGTON STREET,

CHICAGO.

HUGH DALEY, 94 Washington St. Room 26. Telephone 2510. Real Estate

LICENSED REAL ESTATE DEALERS—Continued.

BOYD W. W. & CO. .... 3840 Ellis av.
BRABROOK GEORGE W. & CO. .... 185 Dearborn
BRADT ABRAHAM S. .... 73d and Cottage Grove av.
BRAINERD E. L. .... 65, 232 La Salle
BRAMMER FREDERICK H. .... 35, 70 La Salle
BRANDENBURG & GILBERT .. 503 Tacoma bldg.
BRAY, GARVEY & CO .. room W, Rotunda Rookery bldg.
BREMER JACOB .... 10351 Avenue K
BREUER CHAS. H. & CO ..... 634 W. 18th
BRIDGE REUEL W. .... 912 Chamber of Commerce bldg.
BRINKMAN A. H. .... 87th and Vincennes av.
BRINTON & McCLURE .... 71 and 72, 88 Washington
BRISTOL & LOOMIS .... 44, 97 Washington
BROCKHAUSEN, O'CONNELL & FISHER ..... 130 Dearborn
BROOKS & CO. .... 803 Tacoma bldg.
BROWN B. J. .... 111 Humbolt
BROWN G. F. .... 55th and Monroe av.
BROWN SAM, JR .... 412 Opera House blk.
BROWN W. GRAY .... 786 W. Madison
BROWN & CO .... 316 Stock Exchange bldg.
BROWN & DOBBIN .... 14 Reaper blk.
BROWNE WALTER H ...... 5, 78 La Salle
BRUCE ROBERT .... 62, 185 Dearborn
BRUNER & BRUNER .... 51, 162 La Salle
BRYAN BROS. .... 20 Bryan blk.
BRYANT DWIGHT S. .... 15 Washington
BURBANK & CO .... 409 Tacoma bldg.
BURGE E. A .... 53 Portland blk.
BURR EDWARD C. .... 6805 Yale
BUSCHWAH & FOSKETT .... 538 Lincoln av.

18

GALLOWAY, LYMAN & PATTON, Tacoma Building. | **WANT REAL ESTATE FOR SALE in all parts of the city.**

SIMPSON BROTHERS,

Rock Asphalt and Portland Cement.

CHAMBER OF COMMERCE BUILDING,

TELEPHONE No. 883.   CHICAGO.

CLASSES OF WORK.

Tower and Banquet Hall Roofs, Auditorium.
Phenix Building, Roof, Balconies, etc.
Knight & Leonard Printing House, Floors.
Rand-McNally New Building, Roadway.
St. Luke's Hospital, Toilet and Bath Room Floors.
Laboratory, Illinois Steel Company, South Chicago.
Clifton House, Kitchen Floor.
Illinois Training School for Nurses, Kitchen Floor.

Callender's Bitumen Damp Course for Foundation Walls.

JOHN DOLESE.   J. H. SHEPARD.

ESTABLISHED 1868.

DOLESE & SHEPARD,

PAVING CONTRACTORS,

Manufacturers and dealers in

CRUSHED STONE

CONCRETE STONE,

Crushed Granite, Slag, Cinders, and Limestone for Flux.

162 Washington St., Chicago.

Particular attention given to building Macadam Roads, Drives, Boulevards and roads in new subdivisions.

TELEPHONE No. 1469.

HAMMOND, FRY & CO. | Fire Insurance Agents
177 La Salle St.   Tel. 465.

GEO. S. SIDDONS 48 & 50 Metropolitan Block, 163 Randolph Street, Real Estate and Loans

BASS, KESSLER, ENNES & CO., 108 Dearborn St., Rooms 33 and 34. Real Estate and Loans

LICENSED REAL ESTATE DEALERS—Continued.

BUSSEY WM. H.	32, 132 La Salle
BUTLER G. S. & CO.	869 N. Clark
BUTLER W. P.	461 Rookery
BUTLER & CO	87 Washington
BUTMAN & RICHER	98 Dearborn
CADLE W. L.	38, 185 Dearborn
CAIRNDUFF W. H. & CO	32 Calumet bldg. 187 La Salle
CAIRNS JAMES	1072 Fulton
CALDWELL J. R.	6127 Sheridan av. Woodlawn Park
CALKINS CHAS. R	209 Opera House blk.
CALMANN & FLORA	Stafford House
CAMERON D. F.	220, 164 Dearborn
CAMPBELL JAMES B.	510 Chamber of Commerce bldg.
CAMPBELL MELVIN B.	4827 W. Indiana
CANFIELD E. L.	164 Randolph
CARLISLE W. G.	40 Dearborn
CARLON L. A. & CO	2, 96 Washington
CARLSON & HOLMES	19, 94 Washington
CARSON O. M.	44, 115 Dearborn
CARSWELL WM. M.	52, 88 Washington
CARTER & HOWELL	551, 39th
CASE F. M.	94 Dearborn
CHAMBERLAIN C. H.	154 La Salle
CHAMBERLIN GEORGE W	34, 99 Washington
CHANDLER & CO.	110 Dearborn
CHAPIN H. D.	75, 187 La Salle
CHASE CHARLES C	21, 96 Washington
CHASE JOHN J	12, 14 Major blk.
CHICAGO MORTGAGE LOAN CO.	86 La Salle
CHICAGO-TOLLESTON LAND & INVESTMENT CO.	414 and 415, 225 Dearborn

"Q" Real Estate | **GEO. M. GRAVES** 406 Tacoma Bldg.

C. B. SHEFLER, TELEPHONE 5102. N. C. FISHER,
Pres't and Manager.   Sec'y & Treasurer.

THE GARDEN CITY SAND CO.,

Manfs, Agents and dealers in Standard Brands of

FIRE BRICK

BUILDING AND WHITE SAND.

General Western Agents "Savage" and "Scioto" Fire Brick.

Room 67, 159 La Salle Street,

CHICAGO, ILL.

Gravel for Subdividers a Specialty.   Output for 1889, 305,000 Tons.

Wood Mosaic, ...
. . . . . . Parquet Floors,
Wood Carpet, ...
. . . . . . Rug Borders,
Butcher's Boston Polish,
Or Hard Wax.

SEND STAMP FOR BOOK OF DESIGNS.

E. B. MOORE & CO., 48 Randolph St.
CHICAGO.

HUGH DALEY, 94 Washington St. Room 26. Telephone 2510. **Investments**

LICENSED REAL ESTATE DEALERS—Continued.

CHILD GEO. F. 63d ne. cor. Wentworth av. Englewood
CHRISMAN & MILLER..............1024 Opera House bldg.
CLAFLIN ISAAC & CO.....................12, 154 Lake
CLARK E. M..........................48, 94 La Salle
CLARK FRANK E.....................28, 99 Washington
CLARK GEO. R. & CO.................23, 224 La Salle
CLARK GIDEON E..........................250, 92d
CLARK J. S.......................6 Metropolitan blk
CLARK, POTTINGER & GRIFFITH.........25, 116 La Salle
CLARK T. P...............................69 Dearborn
CLARK & MARSTEN...........411, First National Bank bldg.
CLARKE F. B........................20, 94 Washington
CLARKE FRED M......................606, 85 Dearborn
CLARKSON J. T..........................164 Randolph
CLAUSENNIUS H...........................80, 5th av.
CLAY E. C. & CO..........................59 Dearborn
CLEAVER C. & C. S..................501, 225 Dearborn
CLEAVER E. C. & CO..................74, 115 Dearborn
CLEAVER F. W........................3, 184 Dearborn

CLEVELAND & NORTON, 305, 87 and 89 Washington
CLOSE BROS. & CO.........1015 Chamber of Commerce bldg.
CLUTE & CO............................979 W. Madison
COBB GEORGE W......................A. Portland blk.
COBLE N. A. & CO.....................83 Michigan av.
COBURN J. J.........................31, 94 La Salle
COCHRAN & SHERMAN..................48, 84 Washington

COFFEE H. T. & CO. 12 & 14, 225 Dearborn
COFFEEN WM............................94 La Salle
COHRS & RATHJE.........................700, 63d
COLE F. B...........................57, 94 La Salle

COLE M. E........................34, 99 Washington
COLE M. T. & CO......................190 W. Madison

22

C. S. REDFIELD, 620 } 218 La Salle St., **REAL ESTATE** SOUTH EVANSTON ENGLEWOOD AUBURN PARK

BENJ. BISSINGER 122 La Salle St. Real Estate and Loans

GALLOWAY, LYMAN & PATTON, Tacoma Building. | BUILDING LOANS On Approved Security.

F. A. CUMMINGS & CO.,

DEARBORN AND MADISON STREETS,

Suite 306,
Inter-Ocean Building.   CHICAGO.

REAL ESTATE INVESTMENTS.

THE INTERESTS OF NON-RESIDENTS PROTECTED.

We Solicit Correspondence.

E. A. BURGE,

Real Estate Broker.

INVESTMENTS AND LOCATIONS A SPECIALTY.

BUYERS AND SELLERS, LARGE AND SMALL,
FAITHFULLY SERVED.

---

53 Portland Block,

107 DEARBORN STREET.

INSURANCE AGENCY of **HAMMOND, FRY & CO.** 177 La Salle St. Telephone 465

LICENSED REAL ESTATE DEALERS—Continued.

COLLINS WM. T.	25, 142 Dearborn
COLLOT C. F. & CO.	3, 78 Dearborn
CONGDON E. A.	32, 94 Washington
CONGLETON C. F.	42, 70 La Salle
CONKLIN A.	316 Ogden av.
CONKLIN & AMES	**6, 144 La Salle**
CONOVER W. P.	718 Opera House blk.
CONPROPST & SAALFELD	22, 86 La Salle
COOK EDWARD	36, 101 Washington
COOLEY C. M.	6312 Wright
COOMBS GEO.	6 Illinois Staats Zeitung bldg.
COOPER A. J.	407 Stock Exchange bldg.
COOPER ROBERT S.	18, 87 Madison
COOPER S. T. & CO.	11, 143 La Salle
COOPER & BURHANS	26, 115 Dearborn
COULTER W. M.	10, 150 Dearborn
COUNSELMAN & DAY	240 La Salle
COVERT A. H. & CO	**72 Major blk.**
COZZENS JAS. G.	44, 97 Washington
CRAGIN E. F.	63, 185 Dearborn
CRAIG JAMES	623 Opera House bldg.
CRELL C. A.	41, 151 Monroe
CREMIN & BRENAN	142 Dearborn
CROCKER & SWEET	**9, 125 Dearborn**
CROMBIE CHAS. B.	19, 115 Monroe
CRONIN & ALLISON	**718 Chamber of Commerce bldg.**
CRONKRITE B. F. & CO	**Cottage Grove av. and 43d, and 144 La Salle**
CRONKRITE EDWARD C. & CO	**4120 Cottage Grove av.**
CROPPER & TUCKER	511 Chamber of Commerce bldg.
CROWELL G. W. & CO.	**12, 195 La Salle**

24

REAL ESTATE at HINSDALE | **GEO. M. GRAVES** 406 Tacoma Building.

BASS, KESSLER, ENNES & CO. — Real Estate and Loans, 108 Dearborn St., Rooms 33 and 34.

CHOICE JACKSON PARK PROPERTY FOR SALE BY GEO. S. SIDDONS, 163 Randolph St., Rooms 48 & 50.

CROCKER & SWEET,

REAL ESTATE AND LOANS,

9-125 DEARBORN STREET,

Agents for Sub-Divisions at

| CONSTANCE, | SOUTH CHICAGO, |
| FORDHAM, | ROGERS PARK. |

E. A. CUMMINGS.   R. C. CIVINS.
SILAS M. MOORE.   C. O. COSS.

E. A. CUMMINGS & CO.,

REAL ESTATE AND LOANS.

Buy, Sell and Manage Property on Commission.

COLLECT RENTS AND PAY TAXES.

NEGOTIATE LOANS.

CORNER LA SALLE AND MADISON STS.,

CHICAGO.

TELEPHONE 302.

HUGH DALEY, 94 Washington St. Room 26. Telephone 2510. **Mortgage Loans**

LICENSED REAL ESTATE DEALERS—Continued.

CULVER B. F.	503, 59 Dearborn
CUMMINGS E. A. & CO.	La Salle and Madison
CUMMINGS F. A. & CO.	306 Inter Ocean bldg. 130 Dearborn
CUNNING J. N.	40, 84 Washington
CUNNINGHAM W. B.	30, 122 La Salle
CURATT L. N. & CO.	13, 110 La Salle
CURRIER, BISHOP & CO.	623 Phœnix bldg.
CURTIS J. H. & CO	28 Reaper blk.
CUSHING WM. T.	25, 115 Monroe
CUTLER J. M.	24, 115 Dearborn
CUYLER & CUYLER.	127 Lincoln av.
DALEIDEN PETER	70 La Salle
DALEY HUGH	26, 94 Washington
DAVIDSON JAMES & CO.	44, 95 Washington
DAVIS E. T. & CO.	40, 204 Dearborn
DAVIS & BROWN	3, 102 Washington
DAVIS & DUDLEY	23 Exchange bldg.
DAVIS & SON	49, 126 Washington
DAWSON F. J.	27, 151 Monroe
DAY S. L. & CO.	29, 69 Dearborn
DEAN M. D	75, 79 Dearborn
DEAN & HOENER	24, 115 Dearborn
DEELMAN HENRY	1136, 63d
DELAMATER S.	56 Dearborn
DELANEY HY.	218 La Salle
DENNIS, NETLING & CO.	13, 184 Dearborn
DE ST. AUBIN E.	34, 167 La Salle
DE WITT J. W.	601, 85 Dearborn
DE YOUNG B. R. & CO.	101 Washington
DEVENS E. G. & CO.	6900 S. Halsted

C. S. REDFIELD, 620, 218 La Salle St., REAL ESTATE. BARGAINS IN North Shore Property

BENJ. BISSINGER 122 La Salle St. South Side Real Estate

GALLOWAY, LYMAN & PATTON, Tacoma Building. | **REAL ESTATE** BOUGHT and SOLD ON COMMISSION.

H. M. Elliott.   J. A. Mahon.

Elliott, Mahon & Co.,

Real Estate, Loans

and Investments,

85 Dearborn Street, Chicago,

Rooms 201, 202 and 203.

C. H. EULETTE & CO.,

167 DEARBORN ST.

Branch Office, Corner Halsted and 71st Streets.

REAL ESTATE AND LOANS.

A FINE LIST OF CHOICE ACRES AND LOTS ALWAYS ON HAND.

CALL AND SEE US.

C. H. EULETTE & CO.

Fire Insurance. | **HAMMOND, FRY & CO.**
177 La Salle St.   Telephone 465.

LICENSED REAL ESTATE DEALERS—Continued.

DIBBLEE & MANNIERE.................... 419 Home Ins. bldg.
DICKINSON S. E .... 32d and State
DIETRICH H. S .... 16, 116 La Salle
DIETZ J. L. & CO........................... 209 Tacoma bldg.
DIKE HENRY A............................... 10, 175 La Salle
DILLON & CO .... 402, 167 Dearborn
DOGGETT BROS. 305 Stock Exchange bldg.
DOLAN T. J................................... 8, 168 Washington
DOLAND F. H. & CO. 31, 126 Washington
DONNELLY J. H............................. 4, 116 La Salle
DONNERSBERGER JOS.... ......409 R. E. Board bldg.
DOOLEY JOHN W. & CO........ Cottage Grove av. near 67th
DORN C. E. .... 56, 149 La Salle
DOSE C. P. & CO .... 170 Washington
DOTY BROS. & CO. Madison sw. cor. Ashland av.
DOW WM. C................................. 20 Tribune bldg.
DOWDELL G. W............................ 10, 196 La Salle
DRAKE ISAAC & CO....................... 6308 Wentworth av.
DRAY WALTER S...... 21, 115 Dearborn
DREMALLA L................................. 1367 W. North av.
DRURY BROS .... 1110 Tacoma bldg.
DUBACH & BUCKINGHAM............... 12, 155 La Salle
DUDEK JAS. E............................... 8734 Commercial av.
DUFFY T. J. JR. & CO. 310, 167 Dearborn
DUNLAP SIMPSON.......................... 620, 164 Dearborn
DUNNING ANDREW ..... 23, 94 La Salle
DURHAM ALBERT........................... 179 La Salle
DWIGGINS JAY & CO....... 409 Chamber of Commerce bldg.
DWYER & CO. 646 Chamber of Commerce bldg.
EARL J. H................................... 92, 115 Dearborn

28

"Q" Real Estate | GEO. M. GRAVES
406 Tacoma Bldg.

JNO. J. KERRIGAN,
Real Estate and Loans

518 Inter Ocean Building,

Madison and Dearborn Sts.,

TELEPHONE 2137.   CHICAGO.

SPECIAL ATTENTION GIVEN TO INTERESTS
OF NON-RESIDENTS.

Taxes Paid and Assessments Adjusted.

J. S. MECKLING & CO.

Real Estate Agents

101 Washington Street,

Room 3   CHICAGO, ILL.

HUGH DALEY, 94 Washington St. Room 26. Telephone 2510. **Property Rented**

C. S. REDFIELD, 620 / 622 } 218 La Salle Street, — DEALER IN — South Evanston Real Estate

BENJ. BISSINGER, 122 La Salle St. Real Estate and Loans

LICENSED REAL ESTATE DEALERS—Continued.

EASTMAN H. B.	614 Tacoma bldg.
EBERHART L. & SON.	C. Portland blk.

EDGEWORTH BROS. & CO.....suite 17, 51–53 Dearborn

EDWARDS & CO.	788 Lincoln av.
EDWARS & COLBURN.	9145 Commercial av.

EGGLESTON, MALLETTE & BROWNELL, 207 Tacoma bldg.

EHLERT & CO.	25, 175 Dearborn
EICH M. J.	150 Washington
EICHBERG MAX.	15, 116 La Salle
ELDER ROBERT S.	10, 110 Dearborn
ELIEST I. W. D	532 W. Madison
ELLIOT FRANK M.	18, 132 La Salle

ELLIOTT, MAHON & CO. 202, 85 Dearborn

ELLIS JOHN A ....97, 161 La Salle

EMERY FRANKLIN	16, 84 La Salle
EMORY GEORGE A.	125 Dearborn
ENGERS, COOK & HOLINGER.	167 Washington
EPPS FRANK P.	25, 107 Dearborn
EPSTEIN J. J	21, 97 Washington
ERICKSON EDWARD H.	6155 Wentworth av.
ERNST & SCHMITZ.	271 North av.
ERSKINE D. M. JR. & CO.	166 La Salle

EULETTE C. H. & CO..705, 167 Dearborn

EVANS W. N	3, 53 Dearborn
EVART & WALSH.	28, 153 Monroe
FABIAN VACLAV Q	25th and Whipple
FADNER GEO. M. & CO.	159 La Salle
FAKE F. L.	11, 94 Washington

FARLIN J. W ....2, 85 Washington

FAYE & VERCOE, 31, 115 Dearborn, branch 7008 Stony Island av.

30

GALLOWAY, LYMAN & PATTON, Tacoma Building. | **Mortgage Loans FOR SALE**

EGGLESTON, MALLETTE & BROWNELL,

REAL ESTATE

AND LOANS

Owners of Eggleston and Auburn Park Realty.

CHOICE SUBURBAN PROPERTY
A SPECIALTY.

STREET CONTRACTORS

Manufacturers and dealers in

Crushed Stone, Concrete Stone, Etc.,

— Particular attention given to building —

Macadam Roads, Drives and Boulevards.

Will take the Entire Contract for Platting and putting in all Improvements in new Subdivisions.

OFFICES:

Room 207, Tacoma Bldg.,   Room 600, Royal Ins. Bldg.,
TELEPHONE 44.   **TELEPHONE 1602.**

British America Assurance Co. (Toronto, Can.)
HAMMOND, FRY & CO., Agents, 177 La Salle St.   Tel. 465.

LICENSED REAL ESTATE DEALERS—Continued.

FARMERS TRUST CO.	112 Dearborn
FARRAR J. H. & CO	116 La Salle
FARWELL W. T. & CO.	908 Opera House blk.
FEE FRED I. & CO	35, 95 Washington
FELLOWS & McCANN	2222 Indiana av.
FERGUSON BENBOW B.	70, 175 Dearborn
FERRIMAN R. & CO.	16, 196 La Salle
FINDLAY JOHN & CO.	645, 63d
FINK JOHN	1812 Clark
FIRTH & COCHRAN	47, 90 Washington
FISHELL ALBERT	668, 218 La Salle
FLAVIN T.	Stuart av. and 59th
FLEMING J. C. & CO.	19, 143 La Salle
FLEMING WILLIAM H.	25, 107 Dearborn
FOLLINGER J. M.	736 W. Division
FORCE & HEYL	573 Rookery bldg.
FORD CLARENCE S.	71st and Stony Island av.
FORD HORACE R.	270 Wabash av.
FORD J. R.	75th and Brooks
FORD & LATIMER	54, 94 La Salle
FORSYTH & ALLEN	28, 84 La Salle
FOSTER GEO. S	703, 59 Dearborn
FOX BROS.	1367 Madison
FOX F. M. & CO.	105, 5th av.
FOX, SHEPHERD & CO.	215, 85 Dearborn
FRANCIS, GOODING & CO.	29, 78 Dearborn
FRANK FRED G. & BRO.	99 Washington
FRANKL KARL H.	520 W. 18th
FRANKLIN L.	204 La Salle
FRANTZEN FRITZ	296 Milwaukee av.
FREDENHAGEN V. JR.	216 La Salle
FREIBERGER L. H.	43, 170 La Salle
FREY & SCHLUND	9233 Commercial av.
FRICKE BROS. & CO.	16, 163 Randolph

BASS, KESSLER, ENNES & CO. 108 Dearborn St. Rooms 33 and 34. OWNERS OF Austin Park Property

REAL ESTATE AND LOANS—GEO. S. SIDDONS, 48 & 50 Metropolitan Blk, 163 Randolph Street.

REAL ESTATE at HINSDALE | GEO. M. GRAVES 406 Tacoma Building.

B. F. CRONKRITE.   W. E. W. JOHNSON.

B. F. CRONKRITE & CO.

GENERAL

Real Estate Agency

RENTING,

Loans and Insurance.

OFFICES: { COTTAGE GROVE AVE. AND 43rd ST.
         { 144 LA SALLE STREET.

CHICAGO, ILL.

HUGH DALEY, 94 Washington St. Room 26. Telephone 2510. **Real Estate**

LICENSED REAL ESTATE DEALERS—Continued.

FRIED B. & CO	43, 169 La Salle
FRIEND B. & CO	85, 230 La Salle
FRITZE FERDINAND A. JR	749 Wells
FRYE W. A. & CO	9, 159 Washington
FUERSTENBERG A	438 Milwaukee av.
FULLER E. A. & CO	317, 87 Washington
FULLER WILLIAM G	23, 177 La Salle
FURBUSH P. C & CO	543 Armitage av.
GALLISTEL M. W	Avenue K and 106th

GALLOWAY, LYMAN & PATTON,
1213 Tacoma bldg.

GARDINER G. M	Lake nw. cor. Jefferson
GARLICK H. M	23, 84 Washington

GARNETT WM. & CO ...... 1, 77 **Clark**

GASSETTE NORMAN T. & CO	110 Dearborn
GAYLORD F	31, 175 Dearborn
GEHR ARTHUR C. & CO	114 Dearborn
GEHRKE F. C	1228 Milwaukee av.
GEHRKE & SCHULDT	Western & Milwaukee avs.
GELLNER & CO	23, 80 Madison
GEORGE P. A	53 Reaper blk.

GEORGE & WANNER, 17, 145 La Salle

GETCHELL, BARNEY & CO. 407 Tacoma bldg.

GIBBS F. C	153 La Salle
GIBBS O. F	516, 87 Dearborn
GIDDINGS L. R	220 Chamber of Commerce bldg.
GILBERT CHARLES J	138 La Salle
GILBERT CHARLES T	540 Rookery
GILBERT L. A	713 Tacoma bldg.

GILLILAND L. O ... 38 and 40, 80 Dearborn

GIVEN & JAMES	608 Chamber of Commerce bldg.
GLEASON BROS	906 Tacoma bldg.

34

GALLOWAY, LYMAN & PATTON, Tacoma Building. | **WANT REAL ESTATE** FOR SALE in all parts of the city.

C. S. REDFIELD, 620 / 622 218 La Salle St., NORTH SHORE Residence or Business Property For Use or Investments.

SOUTH SIDE REAL ESTATE 122 La Salle St. BENJ. BISSINGER

LOANS AND INSURANCE.   TELEPHONE 296.

D. W. SHEA,
REAL ESTATE AND RENTING

(Acres a Specialty,)

97 CLARK STREET,

CHICAGO, ILL.

ROOM 22.

Cleveland & Norton,

REAL ESTATE,

United States Express Company Building,

87 & 89 Washington St.,

Rooms 303, 304 & 305.   CHICAGO.

HAMMOND, FRY & CO. Fire Insurance Agents
177 La Salle St.   Tel. 465.

LICENSED REAL ESTATE DEALERS—Continued.

GLENDE CHARLES H................	1105 Milwaukee av.
GLORE N. S. & CO................	9, 79 Dearborn
GOLDY H. I.....................	305 Tacoma bldg.
GOLSEN & CODY..................	912 Tacoma bldg.
GOOD M. G. & CO................	1638 W. Harrison
GOODMAN JAS. B. & CO...........	18, 107 Dearborn
GOODRICH H. A..................	24, 80 Dearborn
GOODRIDGE E. & CO..........	**130 La Salle**
GOOSSENS FRANK.................	32 Fowler
GORDAN C. U. & CO..............	80 and 82, 115 Dearborn
GORDON, MAHON & CO.	**112 and 113 Adams Express bldg.**
GORE W. K......................	304 Inter Ocean bldg.
GOULD JOHN.....................	116 La Salle
GRAHAM W. H....................	617, 69th
GRAVES C. M....................	34, 94 La Salle
GRAVES GEO. M..............	**406 Tacoma bldg.**
GRAY ADOLPH................	**77 Clark**
GREEN F. W.....................	15 Borden blk.
GREEN & TYRELL.................	4229 Cottage Grove av.
GREENEBAUM HARRY...............	2, 79 Dearborn
GREENEBAUM SONS................	116 La Salle
GREGORY & NELSON...............	357 Wells
GRIFFIN & DWIGHT.	**155 La Salle and Washington ne. cor. Halsted**
GRIFFITH & ALLEN...........	**65, 175 Dearborn**
GRIFFITH & DE TAMBLE...........	710 Chamber of Commerce bldg.
GROSS S. E.................	**Dearborn se. cor. Randolph**
GUNN ALEX H....................	79 Kinzie
GUNN WALTER C. & CO............	518, 87 Washington
GUNZENHAUSER JOHN..........	**38 Clark**
GUTHRIE W..................	**12 Meth. Ch. blk.**

PULLMAN PROPERTY FOR SALE BY OWNERS.

BASS, KESSLER, ENNES & CO., 108 Dearborn St., Rooms 33 & 34.

GEO. S. SIDDONS, 48 & 50 Metropolitan Block, 163 Randolph Street, Real Estate AND Loans

"Q" Real Estate | GEO. M. GRAVES 406 Tacoma Bldg.

ALL BUSINESS PERTAINING TO
Real Estate,
PROMPTLY ATTENDED TO.

W. GUTHRIE,
METHODIST CHURCH BLOCK,
CHICAGO.
ROOM 12.

HUGH DALEY, 94 Washington St. Room 26. Telephone 2540. **Investments**

LICENSED REAL ESTATE DEALERS—Continued.

HAAKE BROS	44 N. Clark
HAASE & ANDEREGG	92 Washington
HADLEY PRESTON B. & CO	405 Tacoma bldg.
HAIR JOHN V	23, 84 Washington
HAIR J. A. & S. G	408 Chamber of Commerce bldg.
HAIR J. S. & CO	412, 167 Dearborn
HALE BROS	**24, 115 Dearborn**
HALE CHARLES L	28 Ashland blk.
HALE F. A	723 Chamber of Commerce bldg.
HALL OLIN H. & CO	6, 153 La Salle
HALL THORNTON	710 Tacoma bldg.
HALLES H. H	1 Standard Theatre bldg.
HALSEY & LEE	92 Washington
HAMBLETON C J. & CO	12, 95 Clark
HAMILTON D. G	10-45, 94 Washington
HAMILTON J. G	48, 162 Washington
HAMILTON W. R	**5, 80 Dearborn**
HAMMEL & LANG	**32 Times bldg.**
HAMMETT E	15, 106 Washington
HAMMOND C. G	165 Jackson
HAMMOND C. L	**12, 116 La Salle**
HAMPTON & CO	82, 119 and 121 La Salle
HANCOCK E. & CO	1, 195 La Salle
HANCOCK & HEINER	20, 84 La Salle
HAND J. P	163 Randolph
HANSBROUGH WM	**29 Montauk blk.**
HANSEN H. C	410, 59 Dearborn
HANSON MARTIN A	92d ne. cor. Commercial av.
HARADEN PARKER	86, 170 La Salle
HARING L. W	242 S. Water
HARLOW GEO H. & CO	609, 87 Washington
HARMON CHAS. S	620 First National Bank bldg.
HARNEY & SON	95 Dearborn

38

GALLOWAY, LYMAN & PATTON, Tacoma Building. | **BUILDING LOANS** On Approved Security.

C. S. REDFIELD, 620, 622, 218 La Salle St., **REAL ESTATE** SOUTH EVANSTON ENGLEWOOD AUBURN PARK

BENJ. BISSINGER 122 La Salle St. **Real Estate and Loans**

J. D. ALLEN.   R. H. OPDYKE.   W. G. ALLEN.

ALLEN, OPDYKE & ALLEN,

Real Estate and Loans

Rooms 29-30 Montauk Block, 115 Monroe St.

TELEPHONE 2797.

Refer by permission to
Lyman J. Gage, First Nat. Bank, Chicago.
Logan C. Murray, U. S. Nat. Bank, N. Y.
H. M. Burford, Bank of Commerce, Louisville.

CHICAGO, ILL.

ESTABLISHED 1860.

WM. HANSBROUGH,

115 Monroe Street, Room 29, Montauk Block,

CHICAGO, ILL.

REAL ESTATE, LOANS, COLLECTIONS MADE, TAXES PAID.

TELEPHONE 2797.

INSURANCE AGENCY OF **HAMMOND, FRY & CO.** 177 La Salle St. Telephone 465

LICENSED REAL ESTATE DEALERS—Continued.

HARNSTROM, OLSON & CO.	116 La Salle
HARRINGTON, FRENCH & CROSBIE	213 Inter Ocean bldg.
HARRISON BROS	**121 La Salle**
HARROWER & MUIR	23, 164 La Salle
HART EMIL	301 Stock Exchange bldg.
HARTMAN I. A. & CO.	725 Opera House bldg.
HARVEY JAMES D.	6740 State
HARVEY J. D. & CO.	113 Monroe
HASTINGS JAS. T.	667, 37th
HATHEWAY FRANKLIN	185 Dearborn
HATTERMAN W. E.	768 Milwaukee av.
HAUSSNER CHARLES	409 Clybourn av.
HAWKINS FRANK P.	20, 90 La Salle
HAWLEY E. S	**19, 101 Washington**
HAYNES P. F. & CO.	883 Lincoln av.
HAZLE HENRY & CO.	53, 88 Washington
HAZELWOOD & WRIGHT	706 Chamber of Commerce bldg.
HEAD B. F. & CO	**703, 167 Dearborn**
HEAD E. T. & CO.	1113 Tacoma bldg.
HEATON E. S.	58, 204 Dearborn
HECKMAN A. R. & CO	21, 79 Dearborn
HEDENBERG JOHN W.	6, 102 Washington
HEILE ADOLPH	34, 94 Washington
HEISEN C. C.	320 Dearborn
HEITMAN JOHN	33, 79 Dearborn
HELMER & FRANK	66, 90 Washington
HEMINGWAY A. T	**59, 187 La Salle**
HEMSTREET F. E. & CO.	**15, 116 La Salle**
HENROTIN CHARLES	169 Dearborn
HEPER & MUELLER	22, 175 La Salle
HERBERT A.	4, 78 La Salle
HERDIEN & HOFFLUND	153 Randolph
HERRMANN E. F.	350 Clybourn av.

PULLMAN PROPERTY OWNERS OF **BASS, KESSLER, ENNES & CO.** 108 Dearborn St., Rooms 33 & 34.

CHOICE JACKSON PARK PROPERTY FOR SALE BY **GEO. S. SIDDONS** 163 Randolph St., Rooms 48 & 50.

REAL ESTATE at **HINSDALE** | **GEO. M. GRAVES** 406 Tacoma Building.

L. J. HAMMEL.   CHAS. A. LANG.

Hammel & Lang,

Real Estate, Loan and Renting Agents,

ROOM 32, TIMES BUILDING,

North-West Cor. Washington St. and Fifth Ave.

BUY AND SELL REAL ESTATE, NEGOTIATE LOANS, MANAGE ESTATES, COLLECT RENTS, PAY TAXES AND PLACE INSURANCE.

Special Attention given to Property belonging to Non-Residents.

~NOTARIES PUBLIC~

—AT—

HINSDALE

LA GRANGE,

Western Springs,

RESIDENCE SITES,

※   HOUSES, ACRES,

FOR SALE BY

 **GEO. M. GRAVES,**

406 TACOMA BLDG.,

CHICAGO.

HUGH DALEY, 94 Washington St. Room 26. Telephone 2310. **Mortgage Loans**

LICENSED REAL ESTATE DEALERS—Continued.

HIBBARD PORTER & BRO.	23, 155 Dearborn
HIGBIE DAVID W. & CO.	3916 Cottage Grove av.
HIGGINSON GEORGE M.	114 Dearborn
HIGH G. H.	164 Randolph

HILL A. H. & CO ......4, 155 Washington

HILL MATSON	23, 185 Dearborn
HILL R. D.	21 Tribune bldg.
HILL THOMAS A.	420, 85 Dearborn
HILL T. C. & CO.	58, 92 La Salle
HILL W. G.	661 Van Buren
HILLGER & CO.	34 Wabash av.
HILLOCK R. J. & CO.	22, 95 Washington
HILLS BROS.	20, 107 Dearborn
HITT ISAAC R. & CO.	7, 142 Dearborn
HITZ L. J.	5, 116 La Salle

HOEFER & TORPE ....227 North av.

HOEPE HENRY	730 N. Wood
HOFFMAN A. & CO.	4245 Cottage Grove av.
HOFHEIMER E.	159 Clark
HOGENSEN E. & CO.	106, 5th av.
HOLBECK CHARLES	738 W. North av.
HOLMES IRA	12, 86 Washington

HOLTON A. M ....15, 84 Washington

HONORE B. L.	204 Dearborn
HONORE BROS.	413 Monroe
HOOD JAMES & SON	107, 167 Dearborn

HOOK, GREENE & CO. ground floor, 109 Dearborn

HOOKER C. D. & CO .....41, 177 La Salle

HOOVER L. G. & CO.	507 Stock Exchange bldg.
HORTON J. D.	5545 Wentworth av.

HOSMER & FENN ....10, 79 Clark

HOTCHKISS E. P. & CO.	154 La Salle

42

GALLOWAY, LYMAN & PATTON, Tacoma Building. | **REAL ESTATE** BOUGHT and SOLD ON COMMISSION.

Side margins: BARGAINS IN North Shore Property — C. S. REDFIELD, 620/622, 218 La Salle St., REAL ESTATE — BENJ. BISSINGER, 122 La Salle St., South Side Real Estate

Hoefer & Torpe,

REAL ESTATE, LOANS,

AND FIRE INSURANCE,

227 E. NORTH AVENUE, CHICAGO.

North Side Property a Specialty.

MONEY TO LOAN AT THE LOWEST CURRENT RATES.

F. H. DOLAND.   L. H. JENNINGS,   D. D. BATHRICK.
                         Attorney.   Notary.

F. H. DOLAND & CO.

Real Estate and Loans.

126 Washington St., Rooms 31 and 32.

CHICAGO, ILL.

BIRCHWOOD BEACH and other NORTH SHORE Property

A SPECIALTY.

BRANCH OFFICE, ROGERS PARK, ILL.

CITY OF LONDON FIRE INS. CO. (Limited), ENGLAND.
HAMMOND, FRY & CO., Agts, 177 La Salle St. Tel. 465.

LICENSED REAL ESTATE DEALERS—Continued.

HOUGHTON & HUGGINS	67th and State
HOUSTON & MERGENDOLLAR	137 Lake
HOWARD FRED	615, 85 Dearborn
HOWE H. T	440 S. Water
HOWE MARSHALL K	89, 115 Dearborn
HOYNE BROS	**19, 88 La Salle**
HOYOS ANICETO	215 First National Bank bldg.
HOYT E. J	40 Pine
HOYT J. Q	10, 125 Dearborn
HUBER B. F	27, 97 Clark
HUGHES A. G	623, 69th
HUGHES HENRY L	783 Congress
HULBURD H. A	38 Metropolitan blk.
HULING E. C. & CO	**ground floor, 90 Washington**
HULL D. J	24, 164 La Salle
HULLINGER H. C	111 Chamber of Commerce bldg.
HURLBUT H. A	**30–32, 88 Washington**
HUTCHINSON W. W	**56 Dearborn**
HUTCHINSON & POST,	**56, 86 Washington**
HYDE A. D	10, 126 Dearborn
HYMAN R. W, JR. & CO	184 Dearborn
IMHOF ADAM	18, 80 Dearborn
INGALLS EMERSON	913 Chamber of Commerce bldg.
INGALLS & KIMBELL	**18 and 19, 175 Dearborn**
INGLEDEW LUMLEY	**21, 107 Dearborn**
ISHAM & PRENTICE	**18, 204 Dearborn**
IRWIN WILLIAM E	5, 78 Dearborn
JACKSON N. L. & CO	2, 59 Lake
JACKSON WILLIS G	403, 59 Dearborn

"Q" Real Estate | GEO. M. GRAVES, 406 Tacoma Bldg.

TELEPHONE 1222.　　　　　　　　　　　NOTARY PUBLIC.

M. D. BIRGE & CO.,

Real Estate and Loans,

146 LA SALLE STREET,

CHICAGO.

BRANCH OFFICES: { 729 SIXTY-THIRD STREET, ENGLEWOOD, AND W. FORTY-EIGHTH STREET, MORELAND.

G. W. BOYCE.　　　　　　　　　　　　F. G. KIRWAN.

BOYCE & KIRWAN,

REAL ESTATE AND LOANS,

Rooms 64 and 65 Bryan Block,

162 & 164 LA SALLE STREET,

CHICAGO.

HUGH DALEY, 94 Washington St. Room 26. Telephone 2510. **Property Rented**

South Evanston Real Estate, **C. S. REDFIELD,** 620) 218 La Salle St. 622)

BENJ. BISSINGER 122 La Salle St. *Real Estate and Loans*

LICENSED REAL ESTATE DEALERS—Continued.

JACKSON WILLSEY & CO.	85 Dearborn
JACKSON & MURRAY	405 Inter Ocean bldg
JACOBS B. F.	**99 Washington**
JACOBS C. F. & CO.	187 Chicago av.
JACOBS WM. & CO.	607 Tacoma bldg.
JAMES & BROWN	75th and R. R. av. Windsor Park
JANSSEN HERMAN K.	Lincoln and Belmont avs.
JERNBERG & RYLANDER	97 Washington
JOHNSON, BERNER & CO	424 W. Chicago av.
JOHNSON E. C. & CO	3, 155 Washington
JOHNSON J. W. O	**501 Tacoma bldg.**
JOHNSON S. & CO.	84, 31st
JOHNSON & CROMIE	886, 63d
JOHNSON & McGEE	213 Inter Ocean bldg.
JOHNSON & SAXE	36, 70 La Salle
JOHNSTON JOHN JR	4, 80 La Salle
JONAS JULIUS & CO.	93 Washington
JONES B. F.	6806 Yale
JONES GEORGE K	1011 Tacoma bldg.
JONES & ROSS	30, 97 Washington
JORDAN W. W. & CO.	73, 95 Clark
JORN CHARLES & CO.	321 E. 26th
JOUVENAT C. & CO.	77, 187 La Salle
JUDD J. T. & CO	**707, 167 Dearborn**
KAISER A	416 California av.
KALLIS & COLE	104 Franklin
KEAN D. W. & J. M	39, 99 Washington
KEEBLER & COMPANY	**146 La Salle**
KEEFE T. P	**se. cor. La Salle & Monroe**
KEELER J. H.	423 Chamber of Commerce bldg.
KEELER L. C. & J. C.	5, 81 Clark
KEHL CHARLES H.	21, 179 Washington
KEITH F. W. & CO.	**601 Chamber of Commerce bldg.**

46

GALLOWAY, LYMAN & PATTON, Tacoma Building. | **Mortgage Loans FOR SALE**

A. H. KINKAID,

REAL ESTATE

116 DEARBORN STREET.

Room 31.　　　　　　　　Chicago.

F. W. Keith & Co

Suite 601 & 602

Chamber of Commerce

Building

Acres and Central Business Property

a specialty

Correspondence Solicited.　　*Chicago.*

First Mortgage Loans Carefully Placed
REAL ESTATE BOUGHT AND SOLD.
BONDS NEGOTIATED

THE LONDON ASSURANCE CORPORATION (England.)
HAMMOND, FRY & CO., AGTS., 177 La Salle St. Tel. 465.

LICENSED REAL ESTATE DEALERS—Continued.

KELLOGG O. P.	982 N. Halsted
KELLY THOMAS	18, 162 Washington
KENNA JOHN J.	417 Chamber of Commerce bldg.
KENNEDY & BAKER	212, 85 Dearborn
KENNY & BRADY	33 S. Halsted
KENT WILLIAM	37, 187 La Salle
KERFOOT CHAS. A. & CO.	108 Washington
KERFOOT S. H. & CO.	97 Clark
KERFOOT W. D. & CO.	85 Washington

KERR WM. R. .... 215 Dearborn
KERRIGAN JNO. J. .... 518 Inter Ocean bldg.
KETCHAM S. J. & CO. ... 52, 94 La Salle

KILIAN J. & CO.	4, 120 La Salle
KIMBALL C. F. & CO.	30, 94 La Salle
KIMBALL EUGENE S.	235 State
KIMBALL GEO F. & CO.	300 Stock Exchange bldg.
KIMBLE E. C.	29, 94 Washington
KING S. D. & CO.	513 Chamber of Commerce bldg.

KING S. T. .... 104, 185 Dearborn
KING & RIDGWAY .... 94 Dearborn

KING & TITCOMB.............21 Tribune bldg.

KINKAID A. H. ..... 31, 116 Dearborn
KINNEY C. B. & CO. 49, 204 Dearborn and Auburn Park
KINNEY & KIMBALL, 8 and 9, 108 Dearborn

KINSELLA D. P. & BRO.	154 La Salle
KIRCHMAN MAX.	774 W. 12th
KIRKLAND E. M. & CO.	413 Opera House bldg.
KLEENE JOHN G. L.	5, 79 Dearborn
KLEIN JOHN	148 La Salle

48

HOUSES AND LOTS in all parts of the city and suburbs, for sale by **BASS, KESSLER, ENNES & CO.** 108 Dearborn St., Rooms 33 & 34.

GEO. S. SIDDONS 48 & 50 Metropolitan Block, 163 Randolph Street, Real Estate AND Loans

HREAL ESTATE at **INSDALE** | **GEO. M. GRAVES** 405 Tacoma Building.

S. T. KING,

ROOM 104, ADAMS EXPRESS BUILDING.

Real Estate and Loans.

PROPERTY MANAGED FOR NON-RESIDENTS.

Rents Collected.   Insurance.

C. F. SMITH, Representative.

JOHN KNEFEL,

REAL ESTATE

LOANS AND INSURANCE.

NOTARY PUBLIC.

OFFICE: 360 BLUE ISLAND AVE.

COR. FOURTEENTH ST.,   CHICAGO.

HUGH DALEY, 94 Washington St. Room 26. Telephone 2510. Real Estate

LICENSED REAL ESTATE DEALERS—Continued.

KLEINMAN J. J.	647 Fulton
KNAUER & BRO.	36 N. Clark
KNEFEL JOHN	**360 Blue Island av.**
KNEFEL PAUL F. & CO.	**74, 162 La Salle**
KNIGHT & MARSHALL	**97 Clark**
KNOBLE A. M.	719, 85 Dearborn
KNOTT & LEWIS	9, 92 Washington
KNOWLTON F. B.	402, 167 Dearborn
KNOX ALDRIN & CO.	59, 175 Dearborn
KOBER M. & CO.	94 La Salle
KORFF FERD.	450 Armitage av.
KOSTNER JOSEPH	149 De Koven
KOTZ CHARLES E.	44, 169 La Salle
KOZEL ANTHONY	582 W. 18th
KOZMINSKI C. & CO.	168 Washington
KRAEMER J. M.	93, 5th av.
KRAMER NICHOLAS	5003 S. Ashland av.
KRAUS A. L. & CO.	291 North av.
KRAUTER WERZ & CO.	71st cor. Cottage Grove av.
KRIMBILL ANDREW	Commercial av. ne. cor 92d
KROHN JOHN	457 W. Chicago av.
KROOK JOHN	776 W. 18th
KUEHL ERNST	153 Rumsey
KUEHNAU CHAS	**47, 79 Dearborn**
KUHN BROS. & SPENGLER	1619 Milwaukee av.
KUNKEL M. & CO.	592 Sheffield av.
LAGONI C. M.	690 W. North av.
LAHLUM & SITTIG	558 Armitage av.
LAING WM. & CO.	202 Opera House bldg.
LAKE & LANE	313 Stock Exchange bldg.
LANDT C. E. & CO.	113 Adams
LANE J. R.	36 Clark
LANG A. & CO.	66th and Cottage Grove av.

REAL ESTATE—C. S. REDFIELD 620, 622 { 218 La Salle St. **South Evanston Homes**

SOUTH SIDE REAL ESTATE 122 La Salle St. **BENJ. BISSINGER**

GALLOWAY, LYMAN & PATTON, Tacoma Building. | WANT REAL ESTATE FOR SALE in all parts of the city.

GILBERT G. OGDEN.   GEO. H. SMITH.

OGDEN & SMITH,

REAL ESTATE & LOANS,

Room 60, Gaff Building,

230 TO 236 LA SALLE ST.,

CHICAGO, ILL.

CHAS. D. PALMER & CO.,

REAL ESTATE

BUSINESS CHANCES

—AND—

INSURANCE.

PROPERTY CARED FOR AND RENTS COLLECTED.

BUSINESS CHANCES A SPECIALTY.

Room 57, 125 Clark Street, - **CHICAGO.**

MORRISON'S BUILDING, BUSINESS CENTRE OF CITY.
TAKE ELEVATOR.

HAMMOND, FRY & CO. | Fire Insurance Agents
177 La Salle St.   Tel. 465.

LICENSED REAL ESTATE DEALERS—Continued.

LANGBEIN OTTO T	37, 187 La Salle
LANGFELDT F	2991 Archer av.
LANGRIDGE FRANK L. & CO	31st nr. Cottage Grove av.
LARKIN W. P. & CO	34, 151 Monroe
LATHAM M. & CO	57 Borden blk.
LATHROP BRYAN	56 Montauk blk.
LAUCKS C. M. & CO	513 Opera House bldg.
LAUER N. A	**12, 177 La Salle**
LAYTON R. P	409 First National Bank bldg.
LEAGUE WM	2, 177 La Salle
LEAVENS D. S. & CO	91 Warren av.
LEE JNO. A. I. & CO	401 Inter Ocean bldg.
LEIB A. S	40, 107 Dearborn
LE MESSURIER J	130 La Salle
LEMON JOSEPH & CO	71st and Cottage Grove av.
LEONARD MARK T	**315 and 316, 87 Washington**
LESLIE J. D. & SON	**18 Major blk.**
LESSEY & BORUFF BROS	16 Lakeside bldg.
LEVI JACOB J	236 State
LEWIS & CARTER	6306 Wentworth av.
LILLIG & SCHIMMEL	573 S. Halsted
LINDEMANN C. & SON,	**20, 88 La Salle**
LINDEN JAMES	803 Tacoma bldg.
LINDSTROM C. O	32 Ashland blk.
LINES J. W	1420 W. Madison
LINKE RICHARD	79 W. Madison
LITTLE ROBERT E	151, 93d
LLOYD R. N. & CO	606, 167 Dearborn
LOEB A. & BRO	120 La Salle
LOEB SIDNEY	307, 85 Dearborn
LONG JOHN C	18 Portland blk.
LORING JOSEPH R	6308 Cottage Grove av.
LOTZ CARL	627 Opera House bldg.

"Q" Real Estate | GEO. M. GRAVES
406 Tacoma Bldg.

EDWIN DRURY. HORACE C. DRURY.

DRURY BROTHERS,

Suite 1110 Tacoma Building,
Northeast corner La Salle and Madison Streets.
Telephone No. 2530.

CHICAGO.

GENERAL

REAL ESTATE DEALERS

WILMETTE PROPERTY,

Two miles north of Evanston, on Lake Shore, *a specialty*. It lies thirty feet above the Lake. Have a large number of elegant residence sites for sale on Lake Shore, Sheridan Road and other points. Good class of citizens, good Schools and Churches, Fine Soil, Grand Old Elm and other shade trees. Don't buy a home on the prairie when you can get one in a Natural Park at same price.

A Residence in Chicago for over 50 Years gives me some knowledge of the Value of

REAL ESTATE

In Chicago and Vicinity.

I absolutely control every Property I offer for sale. Buyers and Agents should send for my List.

CORRESPONDENCE SOLICITED.

ANDREW DUNNING,

92 La Salle St., Room 23.

HUGH DALEY, 94 Washington St. Room 26. Telephone 2510. **Investments**

LICENSED REAL ESTATE DEALERS—Continued.

LOUIS JACOB A	509 Cornell
LOW C. H	524 Opera House bldg.
LOWRY BUTLER	406 Tacoma bldg.
LUEBEKE W. F	165 Washington
LUKINS W. J. & CO	878 Clybourn av.
LUNDBERG GUST	59th and Halsted
LUNDEEN A. M. & CO	1, 85 Washington
LYMAN J. F	856 Seymour
LYMAN THOMAS	221 Chamber of Commerce bldg.
LYNCH S. G	153 Monroe
LYON J. F & CO	8, 177 La Salle
MACK & SCANLAN	61st sw. cor. State
MADDEN A. P	1201 W. Van Buren
MADDEN BROS	513, 167 Dearborn
MADLUNG, EIDMANN & McCORTNEY	6857 Halsted
MAGILL J. C. & CO	La Salle sw. cor. Madison
MAHAN I. S. & CO	725, 112 Clark
MALTHY GEORGE K	78th sw. cor. Wallace
MANN O. L	74, 88 Washington
MANNING J. L. & CO	91 Clark
MANSELL & DAVIS	485 Ogden av.
MANSFIELD ISAAC R.	6, 151 La Salle
MARBLE HENRY E	32, 81 Clark
MARCHAL E. A	94 Washington
MARQUARDT A	43, 164 La Salle
MARSH T. H. & CO	204, 85 Dearborn
MARTIN J. M. & CO	108 Washington
MASON J. N	56 Dearborn
MATTHEWS R	707 Royal Ins. bldg.
MATTHEWS W. H. & CO	332, 63d
MAURITZON BROS	12, 78 La Salle
MAY JAMES R	19, 107 Dearborn
MAYER S	North av. cor. Halsted

54

GALLOWAY, LYMAN & PATTON, Tacoma Building. | **BUILDING LOANS** On Approved Security.

C. S. REDFIELD, 620, 622, 218 La Salle St. SOUTH EVANSTON ENGLEWOOD AUBURN PARK **REAL ESTATE**

BENJ. BISSINGER 122 La Salle St. **Real Estate and Loans**

John A. Ellis,

Mortgage Loans and Investments,

97-161 La Salle Street.

L. O. Gilliland,

Real Estate and Loans,

80 Dearborn Street,

Rooms 38 and 40.   CHICAGO.

Correspondence Solicited.

INSURANCE AGENCY of **HAMMOND, FRY & CO.** 177 La Salle St. Telephone 465

LICENSED REAL ESTATE DEALERS—Continued.

MAYNARD E. R.	309, 85 Dearborn
MAYOU J. S.	214 Stock Exchange bldg.
McALLISTER JNO. W.	83d and Vincennes av.

M'AULEY & ELLIOTT, suite 307 Chamber of Commerce bldg.

McBRIDE W. B.	Auditorium Hotel

M'CAULEY & ROSE .... 191 La Salle

McCLURE E. H.	318, 63d

M'CONNELL BROS ...... 19, 143 La Salle

McCORD J. C. & CO.	24, 116 La Salle
McCORMICK W. G. & CO.	2 Board of Trade bldg.
McCULLOUGH J. H. & CO.	70, 164 La Salle
McDERMOTT W. J. & CO.	1004 Opera House bldg.
MacDONALD J. J.	37 Howland blk.

M'ELROY, KEENEY & CO. Main floor Chamber of Commerce bldg.

McKAY A. M.	20, 94 Washington

M'KEY & POAGUE .... C, 177 La Salle

McKILLIP & HOPKINS	51, 175 Dearborn
McLAUGHLIN ROBERT	729 Opera House blk.
McLEAN, BIERBACH & CO.	97 Washington
McNEIL MALCOLM & BROS	606, 59 Dearborn
McWINNIE FRANK	Commercial av. cor. 92d
MEACHAM H. E. & CO.	Pearl and W. 42d
MEAD & COE	37–40, 147 La Salle

MECKLING J. S. & CO .. 3, 101 Washington

MELINS E.	1787 Milwaukee av.
MENDELL ALBERT	39, 177 La Salle
MENGER GEORGE	46, 163 Randolph

MERCHANT J. F .. 159 La Salle (basement)

MERIGOLD WM. A. & CO.	156 La Salle
MERRILL & HOWELL	92d and Erie av.

Side banner left: Real Estate and Loans **BASS, KESSLER, ENNES & CO.** 108 Dearborn St. Rooms 33 and 34.

Side banner right: CHOICE Jackson Park Property FOR SALE BY **GEO. S. SIDDONS** 163 Randolph St., Rooms 48 & 50.

REAL ESTATE at HINSDALE | **GEO. M. GRAVES** 406 Tacoma Building.

Mark T. Leonard,

Real Estate and Investments,

South Side Lots and Acres a Specialty.

Handles Bonds and Securities.

No. 87 Washington Street,

3rd Floor, Rooms 315–316.

Correspondence Solicited.

H. G. TEED & CO.,
REAL ESTATE,
No. 87 Washington Street,
U. S. Express Co.'s Building, Suites 315 and 316.

Personal and prompt attention given to all departments of the business.

Large experience and 28 years residence in Chicago renders us thoroughly posted on Real Estate values and well qualified to give valuable advice to those wishing to buy or sell city property.

CORRESPONDENCE DESIRED.

City and suburban maps mailed upon the receipt of 15 cents

HUGH DALEY, 94 Washington St. Room 25. Telephone 2510. **Mortgage Loans**

LICENSED REAL ESTATE DEALERS—Continued.

MERRITT H. S. & CO....406, 59 Dearborn
METROPOLITAN INVESTMENT CO.
215 Dearborn
MICK JAS. F. & SON..........305 Chamber of Commerce bldg.
MICK & MICK................................701, 63d
MILLER CHARLES & CO.............21, 170 Washington
MILLER TRUMAN F..................702 Owings bldg.
MILLS E. J. & CO.....................350 W. Madison
MILLS C. W..........................405 Tacoma bldg.
MILLS J. E. & CO............603 Chamber of Commerce bldg.
MINER & LISCOM......................9, 177 La Salle
MIZE BROS..........................10, 149 La Salle
MOAK & DUTHIL.........50, 116 La Salle
MOELLER C. C. & CO....................234 La Salle
MOFFIT WM. H........................152 La Salle
MONSON & SMITH, 416 Chamber of Commerce bldg.
MONTAGUE A. J.........................8, 69 Dearborn
MONTGOMERY GEO. F. suite 407–411, 85 Dearborn
MOORE R. C. & CO......................401 Gross av.
MOREY C. J. & CO..................Clark and N. Park av.
MOREY & FESSENDEN......................83 Washington
MORGAN S. T. & CO...............Morgan and Madison
MORRILL D. C..........................3, 95 Clark
MORRIS & GANSE....................29, 94 Washington
MORRISON THOMAS....................24, 116 La Salle
MORRISON T. J. & CO....................162 La Salle
MORSE H. A............................2, 81 Clark
MORTON W. D.........................202 La Salle
MOSHER W. H. & CO.....................346 Ogden av.
MULLIKEN C. H................8 and 9, 99 Washington
MUNICIPAL INVESTMENT CO......First National Bank bldg.

58

GALLOWAY, LYMAN & PATTON, Tacoma Building. | **REAL ESTATE** BOUGHT and SOLD ON COMMISSION.

FRANKLIN C. JOCELYN,
President.
WILLIAM R. KERR,
Secretary.

GILBERT B. SHAW,
Vice President.
WILLIAM J. HAERTHER,
Treasurer.

Metropolitan ○ Investment ○ Company,

Office 215 Dearborn St., - - Owings Building,
CHICAGO, ILLINOIS, U. S. A.

THE PURPOSES FOR WHICH THIS COMPANY IS ORGANIZED ARE AS FOLLOWS:

First. To loan money on Mortgages which shall be first liens on improved Real Estate located in the City of Chicago.

Second. To deal in Bank and other Stocks, Municipal, State and other Bonds and Investments, the Character of which are well known and established in the market.

Third. To promote Bonded Syndicates for the purchase, improvement and sale of Real Estate under the direction and management of the Company.

Fourth. To issue Debenture Bonds, and secure the same by pledging the Securities of the Company in payment thereof, and negotiate same at such rates as the Directors of the Company may determine. These Debenture Bonds will be issued in series, and the proceeds thereof re-invested in First Mortgages.

Arrangements have been perfected upon advantageous terms with the American Trust & Savings Bank of Chicago (with $1,000,000 cash capital), to act as trustees for the Company, and the Certificate of that Bank as Trustee will be attached to each Debenture Bond issued by this Company, stating that they hold in trust mortgage loans on Real Estate to secure the payment of the Debenture Bonds of this Company at maturity.

In addition to the security thus pledged the entire Capital of the Company stands as a guarantee for the payment of its debentures.

Fifth. To make investments in Real Estate, Bonds, etc., for non-residents and others. *We always have a choice list of investments on our books which we can recommend with confidence to our customers.*

CORRESPONDENCE SOLICITED.
(See back cover this book.)

Fire Insurance. } **HAMMOND, FRY & CO.**
177 La Salle St.   Telephone 465.

LICENSED REAL ESTATE DEALERS—Continued.

MUNZBERG J. & CO	282 Milwaukee av.
MURPHY R. & SONS	51st and Center av.
MURPHY & LORIMER	3, 79 Clark

MURRELL GEORGE A. & CO...411, 167 Dearborn

MUSSENDEN & CO	600, 167 Dearborn
NABER & ROBINSON	29 Reaper blk.
NAPIERALSKI JOS	681 W. 17th
NASH, TREGO & HELLIWELL	240 La Salle
NATHAN L	36 N. Clark
NELSON AUGUST	7015 Adams
NELSON OLAF	815 Armitage av.
NESSLER & LEACH	405 Chamber of Commerce bldg.
NEUMANN M	301 Stock Exchange bldg.
NEWBURY GEO. G. & CO	8, 164 La Salle
NEWCOMB GEO. W	771 W. Madison
NICHOL & RYDER	150 La Salle
NICHOLES CHAS. W	15, 208 La Salle
NICHOLES W. D	6242 Wentworth av.
NICHOLS FRANKLIN	146 La Salle
NICHOLS F. C	71, 164 La Salle
NIRISON H. B	542 Milwaukee av.
NORTHWESTERN BOND & TRUST CO	175 Dearborn
NOACK H. C. & CO	716 Melrose
NOVAK JOHN	620 Blue Island av.
NOWAK FRANK	468 S. Halsted

NOYES BROS.....75 Calumet bldg. 187–191 La Salle

NULTON C. G. & CO	648, 63d
NUVEEN JOHN, JR	14, 99 Washington
O'DWYER R. & CO	58, 126 Washington
O'HEARNE W. F. & CO	152 La Salle
OGDEN, SHELDON & CO	32 Clark
OGDEN & McNAUGHTON	412, 85 Dearborn

AUSTIN PARK PROPERTY FOR SALE BY OWNERS — BASS, KESSLER, ENNES & CO., 108 DEARBORN ST., ROOMS 33 & 34.

GEO. S. SIDDONS, 48 & 50 Metropolitan Block, 163 Randolph Street, Real Estate AND Loans

"Q" Real Estate | **GEO. M. GRAVES** 406 Tacoma Bldg.

WALTER H. WILSON,

CHICAGO CENTRAL BUSINESS PROPERTY,

ROOM 7.

86 WASHINGTON ST.

NEW YORK:	BROOKLYN:
Park Ave. and 42nd St.	203 Montague Street.

Chas. A. Seymour & Co.

ESTABLISHED 1841.

REAL ◉ ESTATE

AND LOANS,

84-86 Washington Street,

TELEPHONE 1415.　　　　　　　CHICAGO.

HUGH DALEY, 94 Washington St. Room 26. Telephone 2510. **Property Rented**

LICENSED REAL ESTATE DEALERS—Continued.

OGDEN & SMITH........60, 232 La Salle
OHLENDORF WM. M..................262 W. Huron
OLINGER J. P.......................106, 5th av.
OLSON C. O. & CO........319 E. Division
ORCUTT & BECKETT..........73d and Cottage Grove av.
ORELUP & TAYLOR.................612, 164 Dearborn
OSBORN H. A........................6, 177 La Salle
OSBORNE J. B.....................14, 169 La Salle
OTIS, READ & CO..................706, 167 Dearborn
OTTO & BIRKHOFF.............Michigan av. and 111th
OVIATT F. F.......................75, 161 La Salle
OWSLEY G. K.....................792 W. Madison
PACIFIC COAST REAL ESTATE CO........1011 Tacoma bldg.
PALMER CHAS. D. & CO...57, 125 Clark
PALMER PERCY W.................37, 115 Dearborn
PARDEE H. T....................31, 95 Washington
PARISH, McCORMICK & CO....507 Chamber of Commerce bldg
PARK R. H. & CO..................Halsted and Jackson
PARKER B. J........................5652 Lake av.
PARKER THOMAS...92 Metropolitan blk.
PARKER & McLEAN................517 Opera House blk.
PARKS BROS..........................616, 63d
PATTERSON F. D. & SON................80 Dearborn
PATTERSON THOMAS E............97, 187 Dearborn
PAUL E. T. & CO....................4, 116 La Salle
PAULSEN & SPARRE..................58 La Salle
PEABODY, HOUGHTELING & CO...5 Real Estate Board bldg.
PEARCE M. L......................24, 95 Dearborn
PEASE GEO. D. & EDWIN B. (formerly
Benj. L., Geo. D. & Edwin B. Pease).......404, 85 Dearborn
PECHOTA FRANK J....................386 W. 18th
PEET H. J..........306 Chamber of Commerce bldg.
PEO HENRY C......................445 W. Chicago av.

62

C. S. REDFIELD, 620 / 622 } 218 La Salle Street, South Evanston Real Estate

BENJ. BISSINGER, 122 La Salle St. Real Estate and Loans

GALLOWAY, LYMAN & PATTON, Tacoma Building. | **Mortgage Loans FOR SALE**

E. D. HOSMER,   J. J. FENN,
ATT'Y AT LAW.   RESIDENCE, 68TH AND GREEN STS.

HOSMER & FENN,

SUCCESSORS TO C. B. HOSMER & SON,

REAL ESTATE AND LOANS,

(Handling Subdivisions a Specialty.)

ROOM 10.   **79 CLARK ST.,**

BRANCH OFFICES: { ENGLEWOOD LOTS }   **CHICAGO.**
Cor. 63d and Halsted Sts.
Cor. 63d St. and Ashland Ave.

E. HUNTINGTON PRATT.   EDWARD S. ELY.   JACOB C. PRATT.

PRATT & ELY,

REAL ESTATE AGENTS,

132 LA SALLE ST.,

TELEPHONE.   **CHICAGO.**

British America Assurance Co. (Toronto, Can.)
HAMMOND, FRY & CO., Agents, 177 La Salle St.   Tel. 465.

LICENSED REAL ESTATE DEALERS—Continued.

PERCE L. W.	34, 88 Washington
PERKINS GEO. P.	316 Chamber of Commerce bldg.
PERRY D. L.	62, 191 La Salle
PERRY & MARTIN	44, 143 La Salle
PETERSON, JOHNSON & OMAN	163 Washington
PETERSON & BAY	La Salle sw. cor. Randolph
PETRIE-LANGLEY CO.	48, 84 La Salle
PETRIE M.	163 Washington
PETTIBONE & CO.	161 La Salle
PETTKOSKE G. F.	716 W. 18th
PFEIFFER & PURCELL	24, 116 La Salle

PFLAUM ISAAC ...... 23, 94 Washington

PHARE W. H. & CO.	28, 114 La Salle
PHILLIPS JOHN A.	32, 101 Washington
PHILLIPS MARCUS & CO.	343 Troy
PHISTER WALTER B. & CO.	20, 119 La Salle

PHYALL W. G. & CO .... 91, 187 La Salle

PIERCE C. W.	24, 164 La Salle
PIERCE L. H.	3, 95 Clark
PIERCE S. D.	414 Washington boul.

PIERCE WILLIAM L. & CO ..... 145 La Salle, branch office 3901 Cottage Grove av.

PIERCE & NORTON	12, 116 La Salle
PIETSCH OTTO E.	15, 84 La Salle
PIKE ADOLPH & CO.	7 and 8, 93, 5th av.

PINGER J. E. & CO ...... 28, 69 Dearborn

PINKHAM A. C. & CO.	12, 132 La Salle
PITNEY WARREN F.	69 Dearborn
PITTE ROBERT L.	214, W. 20th
PLACE D. S. & CO.	149 La Salle
POLKEY SAMUEL	20, 90 La Salle
PORTER D. W.	411, 164 Dearborn
PORTER & BILLINGS	57, 90 Washington

BASS, KESSLER, ENNES & CO., 108 Dearborn St., Rooms 33 and 34. OWNERS OF Austin Park Property

REAL ESTATE AND LOANS—GEO. S. SIDDONS, 45 & 50 Metropolitan Bl'k, 163 Randolph Street.

REAL ESTATE at HINSDALE | **GEO. M. GRAVES** 406 Tacoma Building.

R. A. RADLE.   E. H. JACKSON.   D. A. RADLE.

RADLE, JACKSON & RADLE,

Real Estate, Insurance, Loans

and

Notary Public,

State & 67th Sts. | RENTS AND COLLECTIONS. | CHICAGO, ILL.
ENGLEWOOD.

F. RATLEDGE.   P. R. WRIGHT.

RATLEDGE & WRIGHT,

Real Estate and Loans.

88 AND 90 WASHINGTON ST.,

ROOM 74,

TELEPHONE 1159.   CHICAGO.

Branch Office, 71st St. and Cottage Grove Ave.

HUGH DALEY, 94 Washington St. Room 26. Telephone 2510. **Real Estate**

LICENSED REAL ESTATE DEALERS—Continued.

PORTER & CO .... 315, 85 Dearborn
POTWIN H. .... 19, 126 Washington
POWELL BROS. .... 1603 Milwaukee av.
PRATT & ELY .... 11, 132 La Salle
PREBLE & CO .... 512 Tacoma bldg.
PREGLER LOUIS .... 14, 162 Washington
PRESCOTT HOWARD S. & CO. .... 112 Dearborn
PRICE R. S. & CO. .... 17, 162 La Salle
PRIDMORE W. A. .... 4365 Cottage Grove av.
PRIDMORE W. H. .... 111, 115 Dearborn
PROUTY REAL ESTATE CO .... 49, 204 Dearborn
PRINCE E. H. & CO. .... 839, 225 Dearborn
PROUDFOOT L. A. & CO. .... 48, 126 Washington
PRUSSING, HUTCHING & GOODRICH .... 1113 Rookery
PUGH CHARLES & CO. .... 518 Chamber of Commerce bldg.
PUTNAM SAMUEL H. JR. .... 412, 87 Washington
RADLE, JACKSON & RADLE, State and 67th
RAMSAY, DAY & CO. .... 514 Chamber of Commerce bldg.
RAND CHARLES E .... 18, 115 Monroe
RANDALL CHARLES H. & CO ...... 801 Tacoma bldg.
RANKIN H. L .... 420, 85 Dearborn
RATLEDGE & WRIGHT .... 73, 90 Washington
RAYMOND W. R. .... 26 N. Clark
READ ELIAS P. .... 56, 90 Washington
READY P. .... 1009 Ogden av.
REASNER R. & CO. .... 5908 Wentworth av.
REDFIELD C. S .... 620, 218 La Salle

66

GALLOWAY, LYMAN & PATTON, Tacoma Building. | **WANT REAL ESTATE FOR SALE** In all parts of the city.

PREBLE & CO.

510 AND 512 TACOMA BLDG., CHICAGO.

REAL ESTATE INVESTMENTS.

FULL LIST OF

ACRES, BUSINESS, RENTAL AND SUBDIVISION PROPERTY.

INQUIRIES PROMPTLY ANSWERED.

E. G. SHORT & CO.

REAL ESTATE

182 Dearborn St., Room 25,

SOUTH SIDE REAL ESTATE A SPECIALTY.

CHICAGO.

HAMMOND, FRY & CO. | Fire Insurance Agents
177 La Salle St.   Tel. 465.

LICENSED REAL ESTATE DEALERS—Continued.

REED E. E. & CO.....401, 59 Dearborn
REED J. J. & CO.....46, 70 La Salle
REED WILLIAM & CO. 1209 Tacoma bldg.
REHM JACOB F.....204 Opera House blk.
REHM & ODELL.....55, 94 La Salle
REGAN & McCARTHY.....3858 State
REIDLE FRANK & CO.....3109 State
REXFORD E. H.....Blue Island, Ill.
REXFORD & BELLAMY.....20, 206 La Salle
REYNOLDS C. T.....63, 94 La Salle
REYNOLDS F. G. & CO...12, 69 Dearborn
REYNOLDS G. B.....33, 107 Dearborn
REYNOLDS ISAAC.....85, 187 La Salle
REYNOLDS L. & W. F.....505 Chamber of Commerce bldg.
REYNOLDS W. C.....56, 115 Monroe
RHODES BROS. & BOGUE.....915, 218 La Salle.
RICE & CREIGHTON...24, 130 Dearborn
RICHARD C. B. & CO.....96 La Salle
RICHARDS GEORGE W.....281, 92d
RICHARDS M. J.....9, 69 Dearborn
RICHARDSON J. H.....Vincennes av. nr. 87th
RICHMOND C. W. & CO.....28, 151 Washington
RIEHL BROS.....1017 Milwaukee av.
RIEKE HENRY.....169 Washington
RIGGLE OZIAS A.....1043 Lawndale av.
RILEY P. E.....47 Racine av.
RINGGOLD & HITCHCOCK.....31, 94 Washington
RITCHIE & GARRISON.....716 Opera House bldg.
RIVERA T. C.....906 Tacoma bldg.
ROBINSON J. C.....36, 163 Randolph
ROBINSON & BARRON.....57 Major blk.

GEO. S. SIDDONS 48 & 50 Metropolitan Block, 163 Randolph Street, Real Estate and Loans

BASS, KESSLER, ENNES & CO. 108 Dearborn St., Rooms 33 & 34.

PULLMAN PROPERTY FOR SALE BY OWNERS.

"Q" Real Estate | **GEO. M. GRAVES** 406 Tacoma Bldg.

C. T. REYNOLDS,
REAL ✷ ESTATE
LOANS AND INVESTMENTS.

N. W. CORNER   ROOMS 63 & 64

La Salle & Washington.   Merchants' Building.

AUTHORITY ON LOCATIONS AND VALUES.

CHAS B. RICE.   **TELEPHONE 956.**   THOS. S. CREIGHTON

RICE & CREIGHTON,
Real Estate and Loans.

INVESTMENTS MADE,
PROPERTY MANAGED,
TAXES PAID.

Evanston and North Shore Property a Specialty.

Room 24 Inter Ocean Building,

130 DEARBORN STREET,

CHICAGO.

HUGH DALEY, 94 Washington St. Room 26. Telephone 2510. **Investments**

LICENSED REAL ESTATE DEALERS—Continued.

ROGERS A. H.	153 La Salle

ROGERS & BACON, 123 Chamber of Commerce bldg.

ROHRBECK C. C. W. & CO.	122 Osgood
ROSE CHAS.	191 La Salle
ROSE, QUINLAN & CO.	72 Dearborn
ROSENBERG BENJ.	25, 115 Dearborn
ROSENBERG JULIUS.	116 La Salle

ROSENBLATT CHAS. G. 807 Tacoma bldg.

ROSS JULIUS C. D.	287 W. 12th
ROUNDS & CLOUGH.	156 La Salle
ROWLEY & BLACK.	1, 85 Washington

ROY & NOURSE 216, 167 Dearborn

ROZET GEORGE H.	29, 84 Washington
RUBENS & MOTT.	47, 163 Randolph
RUSSELL PERRY.	55, 162 Washington
RUSSELL & MORTON.	504 Chamber of Commerce bldg.
RYAN M. W.	26, 94 Washington
RYLAND & ROGERS.	Ravenswood Park
SACHSEL D. J.	120 Fullerton av.
SAMPSON H. C.	539 W. 14th

SAMPSON J. C. & CO. 196 and 198 La Salle

SANDERSON & CO.	196 La Salle
SAUNDERS T. H. & CO.	511, 167 Dearborn
SAWYER & GARRETT.	89 Madison

SAWYER & M'FARLAND, 5, 125 Dearborn

(See ad. page opposite.)

SAXE & OSMUN.	315 Stock Exchange bldg.
SAYLOR C. L.	164 Dearborn
SCANLAN THOMAS.	97, 175 Dearborn
SCHAAR JOHN G.	606 W. 20th

SCHAAR, KOCH & CO. 2603 S. Halsted

70

GALLOWAY, LYMAN & PATTON, Tacoma Building. | **BUILDING LOANS** On Approved Security.

C. S. REDFIELD, 620, 622 218 La Salle St., REAL ESTATE SOUTH EVANSTON ENGLEWOOD AUBURN PARK

BENJ. BISSINGER 122 La Salle St. Real Estate and Loans

ESTABLISHED 1845.

J. C. SAMPSON & CO.,

REAL ESTATE

AND

RENTING AGENCY.

196 and 198 LaSalle Street.

MAIN FLOOR.   'PHONE 789.

CHAS. A. SAWYER.   THOS. W. McFARLAND.

SAWYER & McFARLAND,

Real Estate and Loans,

(TELEPHONE 1600.)

125 DEARBORN STREET,

ROOM 5.   CHICAGO.

DOUGLAS PARK PROPERTY A SPECIALTY.

Branch Office, Cor. Ogden and Kedzie Avenues.
(OPEN SUNDAYS.)

Also Lots, Acres and Manufacturing Sites at Pullman and Kensington.

RESIDENCE PROPERTY AT ENGLEWOOD.

INSURANCE AGENCY OF **HAMMOND, FRY & CO.** 177 La Salle St. Telephone 465

BASS, KESSLER, ENNES & CO. OWNERS OF **PULLMAN PROPERTY** 108 Dearborn St., Rooms 33 & 34.

CHOICE JACKSON PARK PROPERTY FOR SALE BY **Geo. S. Siddons** 163 Randolph St., Rooms 48 & 50.

LICENSED REAL ESTATE DEALERS—Continued.

SCHACK FRANZ	482 Milwaukee av.
SCHLENKER JOSEPH	55 N. Clark
SCHLESINGER JULIUS	268, 5th av.
SCHMID GODFREY	**610, 59 Dearborn**
SCHMIDT L. F. C. & CO	710 Chamber of Commerce bldg.
SCHONBECK BROS	1205 Tacoma bldg.
SCHONFELD W. A.	42, 151 La Salle
SCHRADER BROS	12, 162 Washington
SCHROEDER & BRAMANN	857 W. 21st
SCHULTZ C. F.	1417 Ogden av.
SCHUMACHER CHAS. C.	266 Blue Island av.
SCHUMACHER CHAS. F. JR	242 Blue Island av.
SCHUMACHER & GNAEDINGER	14, 163 Randolph
SCHWARTZ & CO.	27, 183 W. Madison
SCHWARTZ & REHFELD	41, 162 Washington
SCOTT G. E. & H. C.	62, 175 Dearborn
SCOTT, GAGE & SEARS	46 Clark
SCOTT, HALLOCK & CO.	6, 168 Washington
SEARS W. R.	49, 162 Washington
SEEGER & HANSSEN	659 Sedgwick
SEIFFE & FRANKFURTER	110 Clybourn av.
SEPPLE J. J.	31, 116 Dearborn
SEYMOUR C. A. & CO	**84 Washington**
SHAFFNER CHAS.	165 Randolph
SHANGHY BROS	22, 196 La Salle
SHEA DANIEL W	**22, 97 Clark**
SHELDON & SHELDON	32, 99 Randolph
SHEPHERD C. D.	130 La Salle
SHERWOOD HENRY W.	212, 164 Dearborn
SHORT E. G. & CO	**25, 184 Dearborn**
SHUBART AARON	201, 167 Dearborn
SICKELS & HUFMAYER	695 Lincoln av.
SIDDONS GEO. S	**48 and 50 Metropolitan blk.**

HREAL ESTATE at **INSDALE** | **GEO. M. GRAVES** 406 Tacoma Building.

SIMPSON BROTHERS,

Rock Asphalt and Portland Cement.

CHAMBER OF COMMERCE BUILDING,

TELEPHONE No. 883.   **CHICAGO.**

CLASSES OF WORK.

Tower and Banquet Hall Roofs, Auditorium.
Phenix Building, Roof, Balconies, etc.
Knight & Leonard Printing House, Floors.
Rand-McNally New Building, Roadway.
St. Luke's Hospital, Toilet and Bath Room Floors.
Laboratory, Illinois Steel Company, South Chicago.
Clifton House, Kitchen Floor.
Illinois Training School for Nurses, Kitchen Floor.

Callender's Bitumen Damp Course for Foundation Walls.

JOHN DOLESE.   **J. H. SHEPARD.**

ESTABLISHED 1868.

DOLESE & SHEPARD,

PAVING CONTRACTORS,

Manufacturers and dealers in

CRUSHED STONE

CONCRETE STONE,

Crushed Granite, Slag, Cinders, and Limestone for Flux.

162 Washington St., Chicago.

Particular attention given to building Macadam Roads, Drives, Boulevards and roads in new subdivisions.

TELEPHONE No. 1469.

HUGH DALEY, 94 Washington St. Room 26. Telephone 2510. **Mortgage Loans**

LICENSED REAL ESTATE DEALERS—Continued.

SIEBERT C. A	525 Opera House bldg.
SILVA C. P. & F. P	114 La Salle
SINOLET JOHN	627 S. Center av.
SIPPERLY E. & CO	2, 80 Dearborn
SIVYER WILLIAM, JR	305 Chamber of Commerce bldg.

SLOSSON W. E..........315, 85 Dearborn

SLATTERY T. W. & CO	83, 121 La Salle
SLAUGHTER A. O. & CO	114 La Salle
SMALLEY H. D	718 Chamber of Commerce bldg.
SMITH ADDIE R	355, 44th
SMITH A. H	53, 79 Dearborn
SMITH A. N. & CO	8 Commercial blk. (S. C.)
SMITH DUNLAP & CO	Dearborn and Monroe
SMITH E. N	82d and Commercial av.

SMITH JAMES JAY & CO....612 Stock Exchange bldg.

SMITH K. & CO	321 W. Ohio
SMITH L. M. & BRO	Cottage Grove av. cor. Drexel boul.
SMITH R. B	37, 99 Washington
SMITH TOWNSEND	42, 97 Washington
SMITH & LOW	526 Opera House bldg.
SNAPP C. D. & CO	14, 175 Dearborn
SNELL ALBERT J	544 W. Madison
SNOW TAYLOR A	13, 115 Monroe
SNOW & DICKINSON	Dearborn cor. Washington
SNYDACKER & CO	153 Washington
SNYDER THOMAS D	10, 115 Dearborn
SONNENSCHEIN & SOLOMON	301 Opera House bldg.

SOULE F. A. & CO........36, 164 La Salle

SOULE F. G	221 Chamber of Commerce bldg.
SOUTHARD A. B	94, 115 Dearborn

SOUTHERN INVESTMENT CO. (THE),
306 Stock Exchange bldg.

SPENCER GEORGE W	620, 85 Dearborn

GALLOWAY, LYMAN & PATTON, Tacoma Building. | **REAL ESTATE** BOUGHT and SOLD ON COMMISSION.

ESTABLISHED 1868.

M. J. RICHARDS,

Real Estate and Loan Broker,

69 DEARBORN STREET,

Room 9.   CHICAGO.

Strict Attention Given to Large Business Properties and Farm Properties.

Harold Sturges.   **John T. Barker.**   **Frank S. Betz.**

Sturges, Barker & Betz.
Real Estate.
Renting, Loans.
Insurance.
153 Washington St.
Chicago

SPECIAL ATTENTION GIVEN TO THE

Care and Management of Real Estate.

TAXES PAID.   RENTS COLLECTED.

Loans Negotiated, Fire Insurance Placed. Interests of Non-Residents Carefully Looked after.

☞ We solicit property from owners to subdivide, improve and take entire control of on commission. First-class reference. Correspondence solicited.

REFERENCE BY PERMISSION:

CHICAGO STEEL WORKS.
CENTRAL ELEVATOR CO.
E. B. LATHROP, Cashier,
National Bank of America.

Hon. GEORGE H. HARLOW,
Ex-Secretary of State.
M. N. BURCHARD, General Mgr.
Simpson, Hall & Miller.

Agents and Correspondents of The Arthur R. Briggs Co., 321 Pine St., San Francisco, Cal. Agents and Managers of the famous Fresno Fruit District.

CITY OF LONDON FIRE INS. CO. (Limited), ENGLAND.
HAMMOND, FRY & CO., Agts, 177 La Salle St.   Tel. 465.

LICENSED REAL ESTATE DEALERS—Continued.

SPENCER JAY B	166 Randolph
SPENCER W. E.	1300 Auditorium bldg.

SPENCER & FORDHAM...308 Chamber of Commerce bldg.

SPOTTEN WM. S	901 Tacoma bldg.

SPRINGER C. D........71, 115 Dearborn

SPRINGER W. N. & CO.	5, 85 Washington
STAAB & FLEISCHER	15, 78 Dearborn
STACK A.	300 W. Indiana
STALBUS & CASPERS	28, 126 Washington
STAN T. & CO.	698 Milwaukee av.
STANDISH & SCHOLL	118 Dearborn
STANLEY C. E. & CO.	398, 39th
STANLEY P. E. & CO.	22, 88 Washington
STAUBER FRANK A	724 Milwaukee av.
STEDMAN & CO.	629 W. Madison
STEINBERG E.	101 Washington

STEINFELD L. E.....710 and 712 Tacoma bldg.

STENSLAND PAUL O. & CO.	409 Milwaukee av.
STEPINA J. F.	658 Loomis

STERNBERG E. & D. F. KEENEY...19, 86 Washington

STEVENSON D. L. & J. G.	Woodlawn Park
STEVENSON D. S.	316, 218 La Salle
STEWART G. H. & CO.	95 Washington
STILES & LEGG.	12, 130 Dearborn

STOCK ERNST..............374 Division

STOCKHOFF A. JOSEPH	Berne and Belmont av.
STOKES WM. N. & CO.	9, 183 W. Madison
STONE A. J.	470 W. Madison
STONE HENRY M. & CO.	70, 187 La Salle
STONE H. O. & CO.	12, 206 La Salle

FOR SALE BY BASS, KESSLER, ENNES & CO., 108 Dearborn St. Rooms 33 & 34. City and Suburban Property

REAL ESTATE AND LOANS—GEO. S. SIDDONS, 163 Randolph Street. 48 & 50 Metropolitan Bl'k.

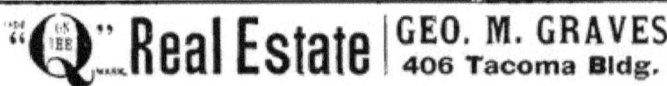
GEO. M. GRAVES, 406 Tacoma Bldg.

Wood Mosaic, ...
. . . . . . Parquet Floors,
Wood Carpet, ...
. . . . . . Rug Borders,
Butcher's Boston Polish,
Or Hard Wax.

SEND STAMP FOR BOOK OF DESIGNS.

E. B. MOORE & CO., 48 Randolph St. CHICAGO.

C. B. SHEFLER, Pres't and Manager. TELEPHONE 5102. N. C. FISHER, Sec'y & Treasurer.

THE GARDEN CITY SAND CO.,

Manfs. Agents and dealers in Standard Brands of

FIRE BRICK

BUILDING AND WHITE SAND.

General Western Agents "Savage" and "Scioto" Fire Brick.

Room 67, 159 La Salle Street,
CHICAGO, ILL.

Gravel for Subdividers a Specialty.   Output for 1889, 305.000 Tons.

HUGH DALEY, 94 Washington St. Room 26. Telephone 2510. **Property Rented**

LICENSED REAL ESTATE DEALERS—Continued.

STONE JOHN N. & CO .... 713 Stock Exchange bldg.
STORRS D. W .... 355 Rookery
STRONG D. O .... 16 Portland blk.
STULTS A. S. & CO .... 71, 187 La Salle
STURGES, BARKER & BETZ ...... 153 Washington
SULLIVAN & VAN NEST .... 711 Tacoma bldg.
SUMMERS & BRADY .... Wilson av. and Ravenswood Park
SUMWALT & CO .... 26, 116 La Salle
SURGHNOR V. H ...... 309, 85 Dearborn
SUTFIN E. I .... 30, 69 Dearborn
SUTHERLAND D. W .... 83 Washington
SUTOR J. T .... 1264 W. Madison
SWARTWOUT T. & SON .... 6312 Sherman
SWEENEY, REEGAN & McCARTHY .... 3858 State
SWEET H .... 22, 94 La Salle
SWEET JAMES M .... 99 Washington
SWEET & DANA .... 404 Chamber of Commerce bldg.
SWEHLA M. W .... California av. and 20th
SWIFT L. J. & CO .... 231 W. Madison
SYNNESTOEDT OTTO .... 163 Washington
TALBOT C. H. & SON ...... 911 Chamber of Commerce bldg.
TATUM L. W. & CO .... 16, 175 Dearborn
TAYLOR CALVIN F .... 35, 99 Washington
TAYLOR HENRY E. & CO. 1206 Tacoma bldg.
TAYLOR J. M .... 1, 78 Dearborn
TAYLOR W. F. & CO .... 304 Tacoma bldg.
TEED H. G. & CO. 315 and 316, 87 Washington
TEMPLETON & MARTIN .... Howard av. se. cor. 136th

78

GALLOWAY, LYMAN & PATTON, Tacoma Building. | **Mortgage Loans FOR SALE**

JOHN N. STONE.   MELVIN McKEE.

*R*eal *E*state

INVESTMENTS.

— DEALERS IN —

MARGINS,

167 Dearborn St.,

Stock Exchange Building,

ROOM 713.

JOHN N. STONE & Co.

REFERENCES.

JUDGE W. Q. GRESHAM.

JAMES LANE ALLEN, Attorney.

Gen. J. C. BLACK.

Hon. J. T. CLARKSON.

CHAS. S. THORNTON, Attorney.

HAUGAN & LINDGREN, Bankers.

THE LONDON ASSURANCE CORPORATION (England.)
HAMMOND, FRY & CO., AGTS., 177 La Salle St. Tel. 465.

BASS, KESSLER, ENNES & CO. Rooms 33 & 34, 108 Dearborn St., *HOUSES AND LOTS in all parts of the city and suburbs, for sale by*

GEO. S. SIDDONS 48 & 50 Metropolitan Block, 163 Randolph Street, Real Estate AND Loans

LICENSED REAL ESTATE DEALERS—Continued.

THARP E. H. & CO........................619, 87 Washington
THIELEPAPE E.........................317 Inter Ocean bldg.
THOMAS B. W. & CO....................34 Marine bldg.
THOMASSON NELSON....................21, 115 Dearborn
THOMPSON C. H. & CO..................806 Tacoma bldg.
THOMPSON J. F.........................168 Washington
THOMPSON, RHOADES & CO..............56, 86 Washington
THOMPSON WM. HALE....................229 W. Madison
THOMPSON & DEEGAN...........704 Stock Exchange bldg.
THURN JNO. L..........................2825 Archer av.
TIDHOLM AUGUST.......................47, 187 La Salle
TIMMIS FRANK.........................37, 97 Clark
TINSMAN C. W.........................412, 63d
TOOLEN A. J...........706, 225 Dearborn
TRENTON J. RICHARD...................618, 69th
TRUMBULL JNO. H......................6 Borden blk.
TURCK J. B. JR.......................8, 92 La Salle
TURNER & BOND.......102 Washington
TURNER & CO..........................170 Lincoln av.
ULRICH B. A. & SON...................27, 90 Washington
UNITED STATES LOAN SYNDICATE (THE)........310 Opera House bldg.
VAIL J. D. JR.......514 Inter Ocean bldg.
VALERIO A. M.........................348 Clark
VALIQUET MAX & CO...................305 Blue Island av.
VAN ALLEN M..........................6, 69 Dearborn
VAN BUREN & VAN STON, 1249 W. Madison
VAN KEUREN C. W........416, 70 State
VAN SCHAACK H. C. & CO. 87 Dearborn
VAN SMITH J. T. & CO.................43 Portland blk.
VAN VLISSINGEN J. H. & BRO...........91 Dearborn

80

REAL ESTATE at HINSDALE | **GEO. M. GRAVES** 406 Tacoma Building.

B. Van Buren.　　　TELEPHONE 7007.　　　J. T Van Ston.
NOTARY PUBLIC.　　　　　　　　　　　　NOTARY PUBLIC.

Van Buren & Van Ston,

Real Estate,

Loan and Renting Agents,

1249 W. Madison St.,

Entrance on California Ave.

CHICAGO.

Rents collected.
Real Estate bought and sold.
Mortgages negotiated.
Estates carefully managed.
Leases, Mortgages, Deeds,
etc., executed.
Abstracts examined.

Insurance Agents.

J. D. VAIL, JR.,

514 INTER OCEAN BUILDING,

CORNER MADISON AND DEARBORN STS.

REAL ESTATE,
LOANS, RENTING AND INSURANCE.

SPECIAL BARGAINS IN SOUTH SIDE PROPERTY,

IMPROVED AND VACANT.

A Call for Prices and you will be convinced.

HUGH DALEY, 94 Washington St. Room 26. Telephone 2510. **Real Estate**

LICENSED REAL ESTATE DEALERS—Continued.

VAN VLISSINGEN PETER......95 Washington
VERCOE A..........31, 115 Dearborn
VINZENS F. W..........9203 Commercial av.
VIVIAN R. S. & CO..........22, 185 Dearborn
VOPICKA & KUBIN......207 W. 12th
VOSS L. C. & CO..........614, 167 Dearborn
WADSWORTH JAMES, 6, 84 Washington
WAGNER HOWARD..........15, 195 La Salle
WAGNER L. C..........21, 79 Dearborn
WAHL JULIUS........45, 115 Dearborn
WAIN JOHN..........303 Tacoma bldg.
WALCH JOHN D..........152 La Salle
WALDEN & MULVANE..........16, 95 Dearborn
WALKER, LARNED & MOSS, 201 Tacoma bldg.
WALKER W. S..........4 Lake
WALLACE W. V. & CO..........1009 W. Madison
WALLACE & HECKMAN..........59, 79 Dearborn
WALLECK C. R..........728 S. Halsted
WALLECK WM. R..........603 Center av.
WALLEN & PROBST, 317 and 318 Inter Ocean bldg.
WALLENBERG G. & CO..........49, 95 Clark
WALLER E. C..........705 Rookery
WALLER JAMES L. & CO..........119 and 121 La Salle
WALMSLEY WM..........5, 202 La Salle
WAPPNER GEO. H. & CO..........94, 323 Dearborn
WARE ELISHA C..........41, 95 Washington
WARFIELD E. A..........305, 164 Dearborn
WARNER & REDFIELD..........6161 Wentworth av.
WATERMAN J. W. & CO..........710, 59 Dearborn
WATKINS JAMES H..........4557 Wabash av.

REAL ESTATE—C. S. REDFIELD 620 / 622 218 La Salle St. **South Evanston Homes**

SOUTH SIDE REAL ESTATE 122 La Salle St. **BENJ. BISSINGER**

GALLOWAY, LYMAN & PATTON, Tacoma Building. | **WANT REAL ESTATE** FOR SALE in all parts of the city.

THE UNITED STATES LOAN SYNDICATE,

CAPITAL STOCK $500,000

ACTS AS FINANCIAL AGENT.

——BUYS AND SELLS——

APPROVED SECURITIES AND REAL ESTATE.

LOANS MONEY IN LIBERAL AMOUNTS

To buy or Build Homes. Payable in Monthly Installments, about equal to Rent.

Attention of Investors is called to our preferred Stock, on which a 8 per cent Quarterly Dividend is Guaranteed. Same is secured by Real Estate Mortgages Deposited with a Trust Company.

Also to our Guaranteed Dividend Stock,

Payable in Monthly Installments of One Dollar per share, guaranteed to mature in six years. Money withdrawable at any time, with six per cent. interest on monthly payments, compounded monthly.

OPERA HOUSE BUILDING,

SUITE 310.   CHICAGO, ILL.

HAMMOND, FRY & CO. | Fire Insurance Agents
177 La Salle St. Tel. 465.

LICENSED REAL ESTATE DEALERS—Continued.

WATKINS M.	38, 90 Washington
WATSON JOHN	76th and I. C. R. R.
WEAGE & TUCKER	1110 Tacoma bldg.
WEART E. N. & CO.	308, 167 Dearborn
WEBER B. F. & CO.	15, 84 La Salle
WEBER JOHN J.	1052, 22d
WEBSTER JOHN	41, 107 Dearborn
WEDDELL & COX	20, 97 Washington
WEDELES SOLOMON	229 Monroe
WEIL JACOB	166 Dearborn

WEINLAND CHARLES, 30, 69 Dearborn

WEINSCHENK M.	6, 153 La Salle
WEISHOFEN PETER	51st and Western av.
WELLS C. D. & CO.	16, 114 La Salle

WELLS FRANK .... 189 La Salle

WELLS MOSES A.	23, 84 Washington
WELLS O. M. & CO.	17, 162 La Salle
WELLS W. H.	302 Tacoma bldg.
WESTENGARD A. A. & CO.	450 W. Madison
WESTFALL E. W. & CO.	130 La Salle
WESTERN LAND CO.	810 Chamber of Commerce bldg.
WHEELER A. W.	205, 167 Dearborn
WHEELER J. R. & CO.	41, 164 La Salle

WHEELER & PETTY ... 505 Owings bldg.

WHIPPLE G. C. & CO .... 3, 95 and 97 Washington

WHITACRE CHARLES C. Owings bldg. (first floor)

WHITE J. P. & SON	13, 95 Clark
WHITE WM. F.	183 La Salle
WHITE W. S.	252, 92d
WHITE & COLEMAN	40 Borden blk.
WHITE & JOHNSON	69th and Stony Island av.

GEO. M. GRAVES
406 Tacoma Bldg.

Notary Public.   Oeffentlicher Notar.

CARL V. KUEHNAU,

Real Estate & General Broker

HOUSE RENTING AND COLLECTING AGENCY.

BUSINESS CHANCES.

79 Dearborn St., Room 47,
CHICAGO.

CHAS. WEINLAND,

REAL ESTATE AND LOAN AGENT.

We give Special Attention to Investors in Acres.

WE HANDLE A NUMBER OF CHOICE SUB-DIVISIONS AND CAN PLACE INVESTORS, LARGE OR SMALL, IN MONEY MAKING LOCALITIES.

Our list of Improved Farms in Illinois, Iowa, Kansas and Nebraska, and especially in Illinois, and close to Chicago, is complete, and those looking for farms would miss it if they failed to look at our bargains.

Write for our bargains before you invest, or call and see us, at

69 Dearborn Street, Suite 30,

CHICAGO, ILLS.

CHAS. WEINLAND.

HUGH DALEY, 94 Washington St. Room 25. Telephone 2510. **Investments**

LICENSED REAL ESTATE DEALERS—Continued.

WHITESIDE J. H. & CO.	171 La Salle
WHITNEY, WOODCOCK & CO	**37, 38**
	and 39, 167 and 169 Washington
WICKERSHAM C. E.	401, 64th
WICKERSHAM D. L. & CO.	56 La Salle
WIESE C. W.	1348 Oakdale av.
WIGNALL T. M. & SON	**303 Tacoma bldg.**
WILKINS BROS.	16, 149 La Salle
WILLARD VAN R.	164 Washington
WILLIAMS DAVID	127 La Salle
WILLIAMS FRANK N. & CO.	19, 167 Washington
WILLIAMS S. LAWRENCE,	**407 and 408, 59 Dearborn**
WILLIAMS V. M. & CO.	**1023 Chamber of Commerce bldg.**
WILLIAMSON EDWARD M.	727 Opera House bldg.
WILLS W. & CO	**4032 State**
WILSON BROS.	9, 116 La Salle
WILSON CHARLES A	**563 Rookery**
WILSON J. H.	313 Bissell
WILSON WALTER H.	**7, 84 Washington**
WILSON & DOW	406 Chamber of Commerce bldg.
WILSON & KEMBLE	83d pl. and Commercial av.
WINDBEIL & CO.	256 North av.
WINDES THOMAS G. & CO	702 Opera House blk.
WING EDW. & CO	8, 159 Washington
WINSTON WM. & CO.	**63d ne. cor. Halsted**
WINTERS THOMAS H.	812 Matteson
WIRT J. D. & CO	3425 State
WISDOM & THOMPSON	6366 Wentworth av.
WISNER ALBERT	1, 69 Dearborn

C. S. REDFIELD, 620, 622, 218 La Salle St., SOUTH EVANSTON, ENGLEWOOD, AUBURN PARK — REAL ESTATE

BENJ. BISSINGER, 122 La Salle St., Real Estate and Loans

GALLOWAY, LYMAN & PATTON, Tacoma Building. | BUILDING LOANS On Approved Security.

A. G. WHITNEY, Attorney at Law. Real Estate Laws a Specialty. Abstracts Examined.	**ANDREW J. WOODCOCK.** Notary Public. Loans Negotiated.

WHITNEY, WOODCOCK & CO.

REAL ESTATE AND RENTING

Special attention given to Collections and
Managing Estates.

Rooms 37, 38 & 39, 167 & 169 Washington St.,

CHICAGO.

Real Estate for Sale in all parts of the City.

INSURANCE AGENCY OF HAMMOND, FRY & CO. 177 La Salle St. Telephone 465

LICENSED REAL ESTATE DEALERS—Continued.

WISSHACK GOTTLOB	4522 State
WOLCOTT C. E.	707, 85 Dearborn
WOLF JOS.	81 Madison
WOLF BENJAMIN & CO.	66, 95 Washington
WOLF MORITZ & CO.	954 Milwaukee av.
WOLF PETER F.	611, 218 La Salle
WOOD F. C.	713 Opera House blk.
WOODRUFF CHAS. A	318 Rookery
WOODRUFF J. B. & CO	149 La Salle
WRIGHT GEO. E	A, 115 Dearborn
WRIGHT & TURNER,	410 Stock Exchange bldg.
WYNN EDWIN & CO	6, 116 La Salle
YOAKUM F. B. & CO	1, 78 Dearborn
YOUNG H. G. & CO.	22, 170 La Salle
YOUNG JAS. T	24, 95 Clark
YOUNG JOHN N.	204 Opera House bldg.
YOUNG J. W. & CO.	726, 63d
YOUNG & RYAN	60, 189 La Salle
ZANDER E. W. & CO	169 Washington
ZUTTERMEISTER H. C. & CO.	818 S. Halsted

BASS, KESSLER, ENNES & CO. Real Estate and Loans, 108 Dearborn St. Rooms 33 and 34.

CHOICE JACKSON PARK PROPERTY FOR SALE BY **GEO. S. SIDDONS** 163 Randolph St., Rooms 48 & 50.

H REAL ESTATE at INSDALE | **GEO. M. GRAVES** 406 Tacoma Building.

CHAS. W. VAN KEUREN,

Real Estate, Loans,

House Renting and Insurance.

ROOM 416, BAY STATE BUILDING,

70 State Street, Chicago.

RESIDENCE, OAK PARK.

Manufacturers

Desiring to Buy or Lease

First Rate Sites,

with water and rail transportation facilities, on the Calumet River in Chicago should call on
or address,

Charles E. Rand,

115 MONROE ST., ROOM 18.

HUGH DALEY, 94 Washington St. Room 26. Telephone 2510. Mortgage Loans

BARGAINS IN North Shore Property

C. S. REDFIELD, 690) 218 La Salle St., REAL ESTATE.

BENJ. BISSINGER, 122 La Salle St. South Side Real Estate

ABSTRACTS OF TAXES.

DRURY BROS..........1110 Tacoma bldg.

FINANCIAL BROKERS.

BEACHY ALBERT D.....319, 87 and 89 Washington
CHAMBERLAIN INVESTMENT CO. James W. Adams, manager. 401, 85 Dearborn
HASKELL FREDERICK T. Stock Exchange bldg.
JAMIESON & CO............115 Dearborn
METROPOLITAN INVESTMENT CO. 215 Dearborn
WHEELER FLETCHER INVESTMENT CO. (THE), 314 Stock Exchange bldg.
WILSON & STURGIS.......563 Rookery

TAX ABSTRACTS.

DRURY BROS..........1110 Tacoma bldg.

GALLOWAY, LYMAN & PATTON, Tacoma Building. REAL ESTATE BOUGHT and SOLD ON COMMISSION.

W. WATKINS & CO.

PORTLAND CEMENT PAVING

SIDEWALKS A SPECIALTY.

Floors for Schools, Stables, Warehouses and Residences.

ALL WORK GUARANTEED.

Numerous References Given on Application.

Office: Room 47, 177 La Salle Street,

Box 22 Builders' Exchange.
TELEPHONE 406.

CHICAGO.

ESTABLISHED 1859.

Chicago Union Lime Works,

F. F. SPOONER, Agent.

Manufacturers of

CHICAGO QUICK LIME,

McADAM AND CONCRETE

STONE.

Room 5, 159 La Salle St.,   CHICAGO.

TELEPHONE No. 234.

EGGLESTON, MALLETTE & BROWNELL,

REAL ESTATE

AND LOANS

Owners of Eggleston and Auburn Park Realty.

CHOICE SUBURBAN PROPERTY
A SPECIALTY.

STREET CONTRACTORS

Manufacturers and dealers in

Crushed Stone, Concrete Stone, Etc.,

— Particular attention given to building —

Macadam Roads, Drives and Boulevards.

Will take the Entire Contract for Platting and putting in all Improvements in new Subdivisions.

OFFICES:

Room 207, Tacoma Bldg.,   Room 600, Royal Ins. Bldg.,
TELEPHONE 44.   TELEPHONE 1602.

GEORGE M. BOGUE.   HENRY W. HOYT.   HAMILTON B. BOGUE.

BOGUE & HOYT,

REAL ESTATE AGENCY

REAL ESTATE BOARD BUILDING,

N. E. Corner Dearborn and Randolph Sts.

TELEPHONE 830.

Real Estate Bought and Sold on Commission.

INVESTMENTS MADE FOR NON-RESIDENTS.

LOANS NEGOTIATED.

TAXES PAID AND RENTS COLLECTED.

Office Desks

BANK COUNTERS,
FINE
BRASS WORK,
RAILINGS,
WICKETS, GATES,
WIRE SCREENS,

Map Cases, Bulletin Blackboards, Elegant Folding Beds,

Of Best Kiln Dried Stock and Fully Guaranteed.

Office Chairs and Stools, Hardwood Interior Fittings,

—MANUFACTURED BY—

A. H. ANDREWS & CO.

215 Wabash Ave.,   CHICAGO.

CHAS. M. BONEY,
General Caulker.

•⎯▸⎯•

SIDEWALKS AND FLOORS CAULKED AND MADE WATERTIGHT.

—ALSO—

Window Frames Caulked and Pointed to Keep out the Cold and Dust.

330 Fifth Avenue,   -   CHICAGO.

COLLECT RENTS * * * * * * NEGOTIATE LOANS.
* * * AND PAY TAXES.   FIRE INSURANCE. * * *

A. J. AUBERT,
REAL ESTATE AND LOANS,

Buy, Sell and Manage Property on Commission.

305 E. NORTH AVENUE, CHICAGO.

TELEPHONE 9912.

EDWARD C. CRONKRITE & CO.,

REAL ESTATE,

Renting, Insurance and Loans.

4120 Cottage Grove Ave., Cor. Bowen, Chicago.

| Furnished Rooms. | Special Attention to Renting in all its Branches. | Boarding Places. |

J. S. BARTLETT.   L. E. BARTLETT.

J. S. BARTLETT & SON,

REAL ESTATE,

RENTING, LOANS AND INSURANCE,

5108 STATE STREET,   CHICAGO.

CHARLES L. SCHAAR.   FRANZ KOCH.

SCHAAR, KOCH & CO.,

Insurance, Real Estate and Loan Agents,

PASSAGE AND FOREIGN EXCHANGE, PRIVATE BANKERS,

2603 S. Halsted St., Chicago, Ill.

TELEPHONE No. 8225.

ALL KINDS OF NOTARIAL DOCUMENTS DRAWN.

Metropolitan Investment Company,

Offices 215 DEARBORN ST.,

CHICAGO, ILL., U. S. A.

Mortgage *=— —=* Bankers.

MORTGAGE LOANS. DEBENTURE BONDS.

REAL ESTATE INVESTMENTS.

Directors.

FRANKLIN C. JOCELYN,
President Inter-State Lumber Co.

GILBERT B. SHAW,
Prest. Am. Trust and Savings Bank.

TURLINGTON W. HARVEY,
President Harvey Steel Car Co.

ALEXANDER C. SOPER,
Treasurer Soper Lumber Co.

WM. R. KERR,
Late of W. H. Cunningham & Co.

WALLACE L. DE WOLF,
Attorney at Law.

TILMAN H. STEVENS,
Vice President Sioux Lumber Co.

Trustees.

THE AMERICAN TRUST AND SAVINGS BANK, CHICAGO.

Counsel.

JOHN P. WILSON, Esq.   NATHAN G. MOORE, Esq.

Bankers.

THE AMERICAN TRUST AND SAVINGS BANK, OF CHICAGO,
THE METROPOLITAN NATIONAL BANK, OF CHICAGO,
THE NATIONAL BANK OF THE REPUBLIC, NEW YORK.

☞ CORRESPONDENCE SOLICITED.

SEE PAGE 59, THIS BOOK.

www.ingramcontent.com/pod-product-compliance
Lightning Source LLC
Chambersburg PA
CBHW020901160426
43192CB00007B/1026